THE
HOLLYWOOD MUSICAL

ALSO BY TONY THOMAS

THE FILMS OF KIRK DOUGLAS
THE FILMS OF MARLON BRANDO
THE FILMS OF ERROL FLYNN (co-author)
SONG AND DANCE MAN: THE FILMS OF GENE KELLY
THE FILMS OF THE FORTIES

THE HOLLYWOOD MUSICAL

The Saga of Songwriter

HARRY WARREN

by Tony Thomas

FOREWORD BY BING CROSBY

CITADEL PRESS, SECAUCUS, NEW JERSEY

LIBRARY OF CONGRESS CATALOGING IN PUBLICATION DATA

Thomas, Tony, date-
    The Hollywood musical: the saga of songwriter Harry Warren

    1. Warren, Harry, 1893-   2. Moving-pictures,
Musical--History and criticism. 3. Moving-picture
music--Excerpts--Vocal score with piano. 4. Music,
Popular (Song, etc.)--United States. I. Title.
ML410.W2959T5   782.8'5'0924 [B]   74-29545
ISBN 0-8065-1066-8

If you want to use this book on a piano and would like it to open at any page and lie flat:
Lay it on a flat surface.
Open it to the first page.
Run the tip of your finger from the top of the page to the bottom, pressing down hard as
    close as possible to the spine of the book.
Repeat this for each page of the book.

Copyright © 1975 by Tony Thomas
All rights reserved
Published by Citadel Press
A division of Lyle Stuart, Inc.
120 Enterprise Ave., Secaucus, N.J. 07094
In Canada: George J. McLeod Limited
73 Bathurst St., Toronto, Ont.
Manufactured in the United States of America by
Halliday Lithograph Corp., West Hanover, Mass
Designed by A. Christopher Simon, Simon-Erikson Associates
Library of Congress catalog card number: 74-29545

CONTENTS

LIST OF COMPLETE SONGS

Following page 21:

I Found a Million Dollar Baby
You're My Everything

Following page 125:

You're Getting to Be a Habit With Me
Shadow Waltz
I Only Have Eyes for You
Lullaby of Broadway
About a Quarter to Nine
September in the Rain
Remember Me?
Jeepers Creepers
You Must Have Been a Beautiful Baby

Following page 210:

I Had the Craziest Dream

I Know Why (And So Do You)
Chattanooga Choo Choo
There Will Never Be Another You
Serenade in Blue
The More I See You
You'll Never Know

Following page 276:

This Heart of Mine
On the Atchison, Topeka, and the Sante Fe
The Stanley Steamer
Shoes With Wings On

Following page 320

Zing a Little Zong
That's Amore
An Affair to Remember

ACKNOWLEDGMENTS

For help in putting this book together I am grateful to a number of people. Particularly to Bing Crosby for his introduction, and to Ray Heindorf, Eddie Powell and Walter Scharf for their recollections. Once again I am indebted to the Library of the Academy of Motion Picture Arts and Sciences for access to its files, to Irene Kahn Atkins, of the American Film Institute, and to Mildred Simpson and her staff for their always valuable aid. For help in collecting the photographs I thank Gunnard Nelson, John Lebold, Eddie Brandt and Paula Klaw (Movie Star News, New York). But most of all I thank the gentleman who is the subject of the book. Harry Warren was unstinting in his help, and I can only hope this book stimulates an even greater admiration for the man and his music.

TONY THOMAS

THE
HOLLYWOOD MUSICAL

FOREWORD

Only rarely do those of us who sing songs have an opportunity to express our gratitude to those talented and colorful people who wrote the great songs which were so important to the advancement of our careers. For me, Harry Warren surely occupies a lofty position in this group.

You know, I thought I had sung all of Harry's big songs, until I looked through the catalogue in this book. I missed a great many. But it wasn't "Mousie" Warren's fault.

"Mousie," so called because of his diminutive stature, is Harry's brother and official song plugger. He called on me regularly, with a sheaf of Harry's songs which he would demonstrate —a cappella, of course—no matter where I happened to be. Backstage, in an alley, at a restaurant, at the racetrack, at the golf course. He was always ready to lay one of Harry's songs on me, and I was always ready to use it.

What scope Harry's catalogue has! What songs! Covering every type, style and category.

I asked Harry once who his musical inspiration was, and he said, "Puccini." Well, there's very little Puccini in "Nagasaki" or "That's Amore," or "Jeepers Creepers"—but you may detect traces of the great Italian composer in some of the ballads.

It really seems to me that that's the measure of a great songwriter—the ability to write any kind of song: blues, comic, ballad, situation, epic, swing, romantic, inspirational, philosophical, whatever.

Harry, along with very few others, has this ability in abundant degree.

I think writing for motion pictures is a special art. The requirements are specific and unalterable, and if the job is well done, the music can make a tremendous contribution to the success of the film. It can advance the story line, and if a hit or two comes out of the score, it will pump up the box office.

The record through the years of Harry's film contributions is most impressive. No one in the field has done better, and the world's musical library has been permanently enriched because of his work.

I always enjoyed Harry personally. He was what you might call a genial curmudgeon, if that's not a contradiction in terms. He often needled some of his contemporaries and derided their efforts, but in a wry and very amusing way.

Harry himself is a practicing self-deprecator. I don't think he really appreciates what an immense contribution he has made to popular music, but I do, and I admire him and respect him immensely because of it.

I really think I'd trade anything I've ever done if I could have written just one hit song, and Harry wrote so many. A genuine artist and a warm engaging human being.

Bing Crosby

PART ONE

WHO'S
HARRY WARREN?

Harry Warren at the start of his career as a song
plugger in 1920.

In the years of the greatly popular radio program "Your Hit Parade," between 1935 and 1950, forty-two songs by Harry Warren placed on the coveted top-ten list. The songwriter next in success, according to the surveys of this show, was Irving Berlin, who was represented by thirty-three of his songs. ASCAP (The American Society of Authors, Composers and Publishers) lists Warren as the seventh-highest-earning creator of American music. Yet the mention of Warren's name does not bring the instant recognition that goes with the mention of Irving Berlin, George Gershwin, Cole Porter, or Richard Rodgers. This lack of identity is something of a mystery within the music business and a bit of a joke for other songwriters, who regard Warren as a genius in his own right even as they make him the butt of affectionate gives about his relative obscurity.

Despite a lifetime in the entertainment industry, Harry Warren has never liked performing in public. "Anytime I've had to do it, I've had to have a few drinks first," he says. And he has no taste or talent for publicity. On the television show "This Is Your Life," which honored Warren on March 19, 1958, host Ralph Edwards asked lyricist Mack Gordon if it was true that he and several friends had managed to talk Warren into hiring a publicity man. Replied Gordon, "Yes, we did. And when the publicity man got Harry's name in the papers, Harry bawled him out. He said it was embarrassing to see stories about himself. And he let the guy go."

Warren had to be tricked into appearing on the program, thinking he was going to a recording session of some of his songs, but his discomfort was eased by a gift from Edwards and his staff. This was to become one of his prized possessions, a framed page from the original draft of Puccini's *La Boheme*, autographed by the composer. Warren, a lover of opera, says, "Puccini's my God. That's my idea of music."

Warren in 1909, at the age of sixteen,
the earliest photo he has of himself.

Warren's primary claim to fame is his importance in the history of the motion-picture musical. No other composer can match his record for the twenty-five-year period between 1932 and 1957, when he was consistently employed by four major studios when they were specializing in musicals: Warner Bros. during the thirties, Twentieth Century-Fox in the early forties, Metro-Goldwyn-Mayer in the late forties and early fifties, and Paramount for the final five years. During those twenty-five years Warren was never idle, and almost all the songs he wrote then—approximately 250 of them—were published and performed. This is unique in the songwriting trade, but what is even more remarkable is that 50 of those songs have become standards and continue to earn substantial royalties.

The publishers of Warren's songs—most of which are handled by Music Publishers Holding Corporation; Robbins, Feist and Miller, Inc.; Bregman, Vocco and Conn, Inc.; Famous Music Corporation; and Warren's own company, Four Jays Music, Inc.—have issued about fifty million copies of sheets bearing his name. Yet the name still provokes a blank stare from most of the public. "This is the cross I've had to carry," Warren says half-humorously. "Even my best friends don't know who I am." This lack of identity with his songs is more of a mystery to Warren than a cause of concern. "I've never been able to figure it out," he says. "I guess I don't look like a songwriter, whatever it is a songwriter is supposed to look like. At the Academy Award show in 1936, when they gave me an Oscar for 'The Lullaby of Broadway,' I had trouble getting past the guard.

"I hardly ever hear a disc jockey mention my name when they play my songs, but they often mention the lyricist. The very first record I ever had was "Rose of the Rio Grande" in the twenties by Vincent Lopez and his band, and they left my name off the label. I've had whole albums devoted to my songs, and you usually have to read the liner notes to find out it's my material."

Apart from his association with the Hollywood musical, Harry Warren is part of a much bigger story—the blossoming of music in the United States. American music was undistinguished until the turn of the century. Stephen Foster had made an impression with his ballads, and people enjoyed the music of the minstrel shows, but very little of this music made an impact on the rest of the world. Slowly people in other countries became aware of spirituals and ragtime, and by the start of the First World War, the sound of the blues began to insinuate itself. Here was a strange new quality in musical form, the very basis of jazz, a sound that quickly spread through the universe. The American theater lagged badly, and not until Victor Herbert did anyone even think in terms of an American musical. Herbert was well established at the outbreak of war in 1914, but what happened in the United States after the war shook the musical world—so much so that Victor Herbert was left behind.

Suddenly a cluster of bright young men with names like George Gershwin, Vincent Youmans, Richard Rodgers, Jerome Kern, Cole Porter, Irving Berlin, Arthur Schwartz, Jimmy McHugh, and Harry Warren swamped Tin Pan Alley and Broadway with vital, tuneful songs that had a flavor and character recognizably American. All the influences seemed to meld at this time—the blues, the Negro themes, the ragtime, the folk music of multiple cultures brought by the immigrants, and the classical traditions and training of Europe. This change also had much to do with the changes in U.S. involvement in the war, the transition from pioneer country to powerful nation, the feeling of new national confidence, and the impression that Europe had "had it" and that it was time for an American era. The result was a new chapter in musical history and a wave of songwriting that was extraordinary in both quality and impact. The world began to dance and sing American music. The time was right. Music was about to become Big Business, abetted by a burgeoning recording industry and a fledgling giant called radio.

Above all, it was the United States' good fortune to have an abundance of eager young men ready with an incalculable quantity of words and music. It was a condition that had never existed before and may never exist again. The waves of European immigration in the late nineteenth and early twentieth centuries brought talent in copious amounts. In terms of music the American Dream was an ideal come to life.

Many of the young songwriters of the twenties were first-generation Americans. Their roots were mainly German, Russian, Italian, African, and Hebraic, all of which somehow blended with the American ethos to produce a new sound. Harry Warren was an Italian with an insatiable appetite for opera, Italian folk and art songs, and the liturgical music of the Catholic church.

Warren was born to Antonio and Rachel Guaragna on Christmas Eve, 1893, in Brooklyn,

Salvatore Guaragna

and christened Salvatore. He was the last of their eleven children, and they nicknamed him Tuti, but by the time he started school the family name had been legally changed to Warren and he was registered in school as Harry. "This was a time when all the immigrants were trying very hard to fit the American scene," Harry says. "It was a disadvantage to have a foreign-sounding name, and I remember that as a child I had no interest in being Italian, only in being an American. Strangely, many years later as an adult I got to appreciate my Italian background and sometimes thought about going to Italy to live. But that was just a romantic notion. I'm really so much a product of New York that even California seemed like a distant, alien land to me."

Warren's father was an expert bootmaker who left his hometown of Calabria in 1871 to go

8

One of Warren's first jobs at the Vitagraph Studio in Brooklyn: playing accompaniment for a film featuring Templar Saxe and Agnes Ayres.

to Argentina because of the opportunities offered by the large number of gentlemen horsemen and their demand for riding boots. He took no liking to Argentina and proceeded to New York, then sent for his wife and children. "I know the image of an Italian immigrant is of a man with a shovel in his hands and a bandana around his head, chewing on a hunk of salami," says Warren, "but my father was a skilled tradesman, and he settled in Brooklyn Heights, which, then as now, was a very good neighborhood. We had a large house, and his shop was on the ground floor. It was a musical family only in the sense that they all liked music and sang together, but we had no piano, which bothered me because I had a craving to play. I've been asked a thousand times to account for my musical ability, but I can't. It was just there—it was like a huge, insatiable appetite."

When he was a youngster, his desire to be involved in music was strong but vague, and it included an attraction to any form of the entertainment business. Warren was only an average student, and he dropped out of high school at sixteen to take a summer job as a drummer in the band of his godfather, Pasquale Pucci, with the Keene and Shippey traveling carnival show. Warren received no formal musical education. He taught himself to play the drums, just as he had previously learned to play other instruments. As a child he picked up his father's accordion and quickly mastered it, which led to his being invited to play at parties.

With his thirst for music, but with no money either to study or to purchase instruments, Warren was lucky enough to make the acquaintance of a barber named Frank de Rosa, whose shop was part tonsorial parlor and part music store and booking agency. De Rosa allowed Warren to study the instruments in return for making appearances as a musician at the parties and affairs for which the musical barber made bookings. In this way, as his own teacher, Warren learned the piano and six other instruments.

In addition to the extraordinary talent of being able to pick up instruments and play them, the teen-aged Harry Warren also found that he could sight-read music. This was of value in church, where he started as an altar boy and soon qualified for the choir. Warren is one of the few boys ever to admit, "I couldn't get to church fast enough. I loved the music, which became obvious to our organist, Pauline Schneider, who took an interest in me and gave me the only musical instruction I ever had, explaining scales and chords. The church was Our Lady of Loretto, in Brooklyn, and we had a beautiful mixed choir. We didn't do the Gregorian chants, we did all the famous masses, and that way I got to know the music of the great composers. I learned harmony with the help of Miss Schneider, and it was easy to sing all the parts. My voice might not have been the best, but I was given a wonderful ear."

The summer job as a drummer with his godfather's band, a brass group of a dozen players who played all the towns in the Hudson valley, increased Warren's determination to become involved in show business. But for a self-tutored musician, particularly one with a quiet and modest nature, work was not forthcoming. He took jobs of any kind to make money, starting with a production-line job in a tin-can factory and then working as a filing clerk with an insurance firm. By this time his brother Charlie was making a living as a song-and-dance man in vaudeville, and one of his sisters was with a professional singing group, but the nearest young Harry came to show business was his odd jobs as a pianist at parties and weddings and being an usher and candy dispenser in theaters.

By 1915 things began to get more interesting for him. He had taken to hanging around the Vitagraph Studios in Flatbush and getting occasional jobs as an extra in movies. Then, Harry says, "One day I overheard three fellows talking about their singing, about needing another singer to make up a quartet. I volunteered that I could sing tenor, which is what they needed, but I could also do the other parts. After a tryout they took me on. They were all Vitagraph workers, and since they needed me they managed to get me a job as a property man. This led to all manner of other jobs, and I eventually became an assistant director, with a little work here and there as an actor."

Harry Warren's first dabblings as a composer came at the Vitagraph Studios when actress Corinne Griffith encouraged him to play the piano as mood background to help her acting. Her husband was director Webster Campbell, and both of them liked what Warren did at the piano. He had learned a great deal of operatic music and found it easy to improvise, which led to his growing desire to write songs. During this musically formative period of his life Warren took occasional jobs as a pianist in movie houses, inventing his own accompaniments to the pictures.

Of the movies Warren worked on at Vitagraph only two are memorable, *For France* and *Over the Top*, both made in 1918. *For France*, directed by Wesley Ruggles, was shot on Long Island and contained many World War I battle scenes. Warren recalls that as an assistant director he had to supervise the many extras. During the filming a large group dressed as German Uhlan cavalrymen rode through a nearby town and frightened the people, who thought it was an invasion.

Over the Top was much the same, based on a story by Guy Empey, an American who had made a name for himself fighting with the British army. This was filmed in Georgia and gave Warren an exposure to southern accents, which he found incomprehensible. The Dixie Division was in training nearby, prior to being sent to France, and between watching them and filming mock trench battles for *Over the Top*, Warren felt that he was in the war. Now twenty-five, he finally received draft papers for the army and decided instead to join the navy, in which he was attached to the air service and sent to the station at Montauk Point, Long Island.

Warren entered the service a married man. In December 1917 he had married Josephine Wensler, the daughter of an American of German extraction who cared little for Italians. "Courting Jo was a problem because I knew he didn't like me," says Warren. "Of course, this was in the distant past, when you had to get permission just to take a girl out, and it took weeks of arrangements to make a formal visit to her home. I managed to win over her father by playing operatic selections on his piano, but come eleven-thirty he would drop his boots on the floor with a thud, and that was my cue to leave."

Warren's attempts to get into the entertainment branch of the service were unsuccessful because of the number of greatly experienced performers already available, and he was given a job as a photographer, although he knew nothing about cameras. "The station at Montauk Point was only 120 miles from New York," he says, "but it was so remote, with sand dunes and the ocean, that it could have been the other side of the world. I was the only one there who could play the piano, so that made me the entertainer. One day a young woman came in with a group of officers, and we were asked if there was a pianist in the unit. I volunteered. She was Annette Kellerman, and she was forming entertainment groups for the servicemen. That made my stint in the Navy more interesting, but I was out in less than a year. My departure was memorable because in those days you had to pay for part of your wardrobe, and my wife had to come up with thirty dollars to bail me out of the navy."

It was during his days at Montauk Point that Harry Warren formed his ambition to become a songwriter. He had written random melodies before, but now he wrote his first complete song:

> How would you like to be a sailor?
> How would you like to sail the sea?
> Aboard a fishing smack or whaler.
> Sailing is the life for me.
> You spend your nights a-swinging in a hammock,
> You sail the sea to see the count-a-ree.
> Sailing, sailing, over the bounding main,
> How would you like to be a sailor boy?

With the aid of his friend Phil Quinn, another assistant director at Vitagraph, Warren was able to play the song for Quinn's songwriter brother-in-law, Al Piantidosi, who had written "I Didn't Raise My Boy to Be a Soldier." Perhaps it was too late for Warren's sailor song, or maybe, as Warren suspects, it just wasn't good enough, but Piantidosi declined to help get it published.

Warren was not to be discouraged. "By hook or by crook I was determined to get into the music business," he says. "I returned to Vitagraph after the war, but things were very quiet there, and very little money coming in. I asked Guy Empey, who was now a director, for help,

11

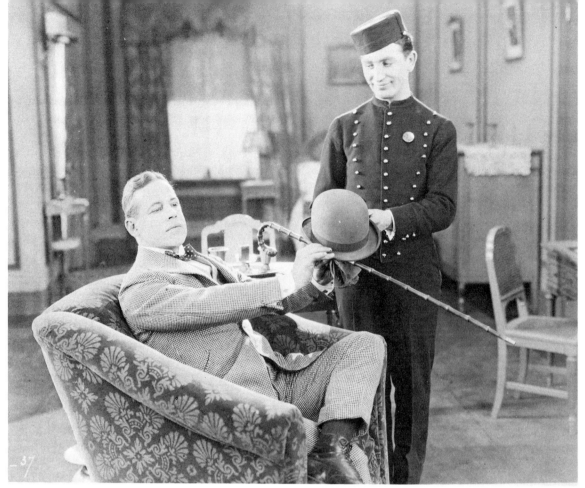

Bit-part player Warren with Guy Empey in *Liquid Gold,* filmed at Fort Lee, New Jersey in 1917.

and he got me a job with The Travelers Insurance Company as an investigator. I could speak Italian, so they sent me to the docks to interview workers who were claiming compensation. What I didn't realize was that most of them were Sicilians, and I couldn't understand their accent, let alone what they called the various parts of a ship.

"I didn't last long on that job. In need of money—we had a son by this time— I took a part-time job as a pianist in Healey's Saloon at Sheepshead Bay. This was the kind of place where you had to know all the ethnic music—German Night, Irish Night, Italian Night, and so on. Fortunately I was well versed in all that stuff, so I kept the job, while trying to write songs."

The first major turning point for Harry Warren took place one evening at Healey's. It was one of those chance meetings that make all the difference to a man's life. Jack Egan and Billy Joyce dropped in for a drink and struck up a conversation with the pianist. When Warren learned that they were pluggers for a song-publishing company, he asked them if they would like to hear a song he had just written. They agreed, and Warren played his "I Loved to Love You When I Learned My A-B-C's." Joyce was impressed and invited Warren to play the song for his employers, Stark and Cowan. The next day Warren performed the song for Ruby Cowan, who liked it, but not enough to publish it. However, he asked Warren if he would be interested in a job. The pay was twenty dollars a week and required Warren to peddle songs to singers and entertainers appearing in theaters in and around New York. The year was 1920, and from then on Harry Warren was in the business he liked.

The work of a song plugger was not entirely suited to Warren's nature. It demanded a glib-ness and an insensitivity that are alien to him. Years later Mack Stark revealed on the "This Is Your Life" show, "At first Harry showed the shyness that has kept him such a modest man all his life. I sent him to Proctor's Theatre to interview a singer. He came back without the singer. I asked, 'What did you say?' Harry replied, 'I said hello.' I grew upset about this and said, 'Well, didn't the singer say *anything?* 'Yeah,' said Harry. 'He said hello.' "

12

Harry Warren's life all through the 1920s was centered in mid-Manhattan, and he looks back on it as a marvelous decade among people he liked and respected. "There were a lot of brassy people in the business," he says, "but the songwriters were mostly a good lot. It was a community, and we got along very well. I particularly remember the summers, because the windows were all open and from so many of them in the vicinity of Broadway and 46th Street you could hear pianos being played. It was a cacophony, but a great one. What I didn't like was having to go backstage and see these performers, many of whom were brusque. They affronted me, and I'd be standing there like a wet moccasin. I was never a great pianist, and they always wanted to point that out. That happened even years later when I was writing songs for Hollywood pictures. I recall one famous producer saying, 'You're a lousy pianist,' to which I replied, 'If I were a good pianist do you think I'd be wasting my time writing songs?' That seemed to confuse him."

The songwriters of Manhattan were a group unto themselves, a separate and distinct colony of men with a strong and common interest. Says Warren, "We all knew each other and the only topic of conversation was songwriting. Other people might sit down to play cards or discuss politics. All we did whenever we met was say, 'Let's sit down and do a song.' "

One of the first lyricists Warren came to know was Scotsman Edgar Leslie. Shortly after his entry into the music-publishing trade, Warren sat down with Leslie to write what would become his first published song:

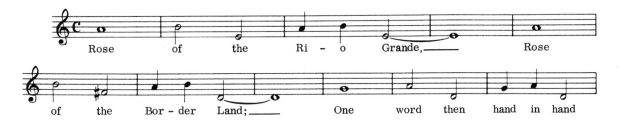

Rose of the Ri - o Grande,_____ Rose
of the Bor - der Land;_____ One word then hand in hand

The song is still performed, although almost always as an instrumental. However, no publisher would take a chance on it in 1920, and it wasn't marketed until two years later, when Edgar Leslie started his own publishing company in association with Grant Clarke.

In 1923 Warren, Leslie, and Clark put together another song. This one, in praise of far-off Pasadena, California, gained considerable popularity and is still heard on occasion:

Home_____ in Pas-a - de - na Home_____ where grass is green - er,

Harry Warren took a big step forward in late 1924, when he joined the publishing house of Shapiro, Bernstein and Company. It brought him into association with two top lyricists of the day, Bud Green and Mort Dixon, and also brought him to the attention of a dynamic would-be songwriter named Billy Rose, a man of enormous drive and nerve. With Rose and Mort Dixon, he wrote "Maybe You Will, Maybe You Won't," which did moderately well and, if nothing else, gave Warren a sense of well-being. It was his tenth published song.

Being able to push his own material along with scads of other songs written by his acquaintances made his job of traipsing around the theaters a little easier. But he says, "It was never easy for me, because I didn't have the aggressiveness and the breezy cheerfulness you needed to be a song plugger in those days. Stark and Cowan made it a little easier for me by giving me the Brooklyn beat, my home territory. There were an enormous number of performers playing the theaters, vaudeville houses, and dance halls, and all the publishers were plying them with

Warren, at extreme left, doing a bit in a Vitagraph picture, of which he can't recall the title. The short gentleman to his right is Billy Bletcher and the central figure is Wallace McDonald, who later became a producer.

songs and instrumental pieces. Even the animal acts needed music to play them on and off. It was an interesting period, but I've often wondered how I got through it, particularly on twenty dollars a week."

By 1925 Warren felt more confident as a song plugger and audition pianist because well-established musicians began to play several of his songs. Early the following year he and Bud Green, also under contract to Shapiro, Bernstein and Company, wrote what would become an instantly popular song, a bright, bouncing ditty typical of the flashy, jazzy twenties:

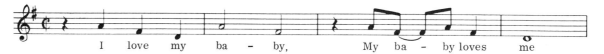

I love my ba - by, My ba - by loves me

Spurred by the success of "I Love My Baby, My Baby Loves Me," Warren turned out more than a dozen songs in 1926. Even though his songs did not become greatly popular, they brought him respect from musicians, who detected that his musical craftsmanship was the work of someone with a genuine regard for music and not just the glib product of the average Tin Pan Alley writer. The solid construction of "I Love My Baby, My Baby Loves Me" gave it durability. And the real test for a song in the twenties was its adoption by the better jazz musicians, whose improvisatory style needed material with a simple, definite form, in addition to an appealing tunefulness. Typical of this is Warren's "Here Comes Miss Clementine," written with lyricist Henry Creamer in 1927, which was quickly picked up and popularized by the legendary jazz trumpeter Bix Beiderbecke, "the young man with a horn," who was to die in 1931 at age twenty-eight. This was one of the tunes on which he built his fame:

Here comes Miss Clem - en - tine_ That ba - by from New Or - leans;_
She's on - ly sev - en - teen,_ But what a queen,_ Oh! my

14

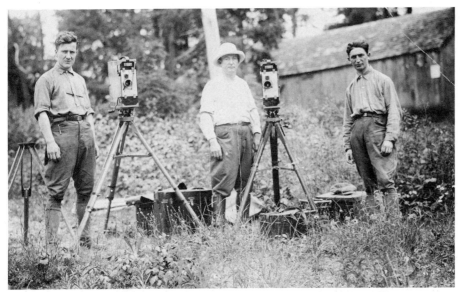

Assistant Director Warren on location in Georgia, while making *For France* in 1918.
The cameraman on the left is Jules Cronjager.

In the Navy, 1918.

About twenty songs by Warren appeared in 1928, the year he joined the large Remick Music Corporation and took a career step that would soon lead him to the top of his profession. By now his income was better, although still not as good as his reputation warranted. Songwriters have always been at the mercy of music publishers, and the bookkeeping in the twenties was lax. Warren claims never to have received any income from "Rose of the Rio Grande" because the publishers, Edgar Leslie Music Inc., went out of business a year later and the rights drifted, even though the song was performed widely. Billy Rose figured prominently in Warren's life in 1928, writing six songs in collaboration with Warren and Mort Dixon. Rose received billing over Dixon, but his contribution to the lyrics was probably minimal. "Billy was a catalyst, and very ambitious," says Harry. "He had some good ideas of his own, but he bought ideas from other writers and possibly appropriated others. He had a compulsion to be rich and famous. That might not be admirable to some people, but you need that kind in show business. They get things going when the rest of us can't."

In 1926 Warren met Al Dubin for the first time, and Billy Rose who collaborated on the first Warren-Dubin song, "Too Many Kisses," with Rose taking top billing. Little came of the song, and Warren and Dubin did nothing more together until mid-1928. They wrote "Then Came the Dawn," which they gave to the greatly popular singer Gene Austin, who published it himself. Despite the success of the song, there was no suggestion of a Warren-Dubin partnership. Both men continued their staff duties with Remick, and Warren wrote most of his songs with Mort Dixon.

The best of the Warren-Dixon songs of 1928 was "Nagasaki," which would become another favorite of the jazz musicians and a standard through the years, although most often as an instrumental. Again the tight construction of the melody allowed for improvisation. Warren recalls that Remick was not much in favor of publishing the song. "They felt it had 'too many notes' and was too complicated," he says. "It's ironic that it should become such a favorite with the jazz pianists—Oscar Peterson, for example, plays it beautifully—because that way you never get to hear the lyrics, and the whole idea of the song was Dixon's. He was one of those romantics who drooled about faraway places with strange-sounding names. I don't think he had any idea what Nagasaki looked like, which was probably all to the good. Irving Caesar, who wrote the lyrics to Gershwin's first big hit, 'Swanee,' said that he and George got to see the river years later, and it was such an ordinary little stream they could never had written the song if they'd seen it first. And I still don't know what Nagasaki looks like."

Hot gin-ger and dy-na-mite— There's noth-ing but that at night—
Back in Nag-a-sak-i where the fel-lers chew to-bac-cy And the wo-men wick-y wack-y woo

The Warren life-style improved after the middle of the twenties. Until then he had been living in a Brooklyn apartment with his wife and two children—son Harry, Jr., and daughter Joan, who has always been known by the nickname Cookie. After he had saved enough from his meager salary to place a deposit on a small house in Forest Hills, Long Island, the Warrens moved in 1926.

Warren had overcome some of the shyness that had made his work plugging songs something of a struggle, but he would never be brash or forceful. What gave him his solidity in the music business was the respect of other songwriters, many of whom eagerly sat down to write with him. Among them were Gus Kahn, Bert Kalmar and Harry Ruby, and the team of Sam Lewis and Joe Young. As the music business boomed through the twenties, the job of song plugger became more respectable, and instead of accosting impatient singers and musicians, Warren came to demonstrate material for theatrical producers and recording companies. "We used to go to the record people and play out a whole catalog of new stuff," he says. "They would quickly respond to what they liked and didn't like. And it was a seasonal business—you had your winter catalog and your summer catalog. It was a bit like the garment trade."

The economic crash of 1929 wiped out a great many businesses and brought grief to millions, but the entertainment industry flourished. The Depression coincided with the birth and rapid growth of the sound motion picture, which opened its giant doors to performers and writers capable of meeting the new challenge. Broadway and Tin Pan Alley were suddenly huge academies supplying streams of graduates for Hollywood consideration, and qualified songwriters were welcome.

Warners' *The Jazz Singer* had opened in October 1927, but it had taken the film industry some time to accept the fact that the silent era was over. Industry resistance was strong. A profitable business had grown up around the silent films' need for music, and publishing houses catered to the considerable demands of pianists, organists, and orchestras in nearly twenty thousand theaters in the United States and Canada. The dismissal of hordes of musicians seemed imminent. Furthermore, film tycoons resented spending the great sums of money it would take to purchase recording equipment and install sound systems in theaters, at a time when they doubted that the public would be able to afford entertainment. Those among them who sensed and predicted the coming need for inexpensive entertainment took a different stand. The Wall Street financiers sniffed money in the air and loaned several hundred million dollars to the Hollywood moguls to reequip their studios and turn out the new product.

Something else was in the air—the need the new medium would have for music. And although many famous silent-movie actors glumly accepted the fact that their lack of good speaking voices spelled the end of their fame, people with other kinds of creative talent realized that sound on film meant new opportunities for them.

1929 was a sort of second California gold rush. Hundreds of musical people bought tickets to Los Angeles. It seemed obvious to them that musicals would flourish first and foremost in this new era. The Warner brothers had won their gamble, and in a further shrewd move they spent ten million dollars purchasing the New York music publishing houses of Witmark, Harms, and Remick, guaranteeing themselves access to songwriters and the profits of publishing songs from movie musicals. Other studios followed suit with other music-publishing houses, and American music moved a gigantic step closer to becoming Big Business.

The movie industry swamped itself with musicals in the first year of sound. In buying the publishing companies, the studios acquired the rights to their catalogs, and among Remick's publications was the score to the Rodgers and Hart Broadway musical *Spring Is Here*. The show had been a modest success early in 1929, owing to its charming score and not to its frothy plot about the love of two boys for the same girl.

In making it into a film, Warners starred Alexander Gray, Bernice Claire, and Lawrence Gray. They sent Harry Warren, Sam Lewis, and Joe Young to Hollywood to write additional songs. Of the original score Warners kept only the title song, "Yours Sincerely," and "With a Song in My Heart." This puzzles Warren, who says, "I couldn't figure out why they would buy a Broadway musical, dump most of the songs, and ask us to write new ones. The reason was that there was more money for the studio in pushing the hit songs from the original and trying to get some new hits to go along with them. People were always asking that same question, all through the years of the movie musicals. It was just that the studios owned the publishing houses, which the public didn't seem to realize, just as they owned chains of theaters and radio stations. I could never understand the business manipulations of the picture business, or any other for that matter. All I knew how to do was write songs."

Warren and his lyricists turned out six new songs for *Spring Is Here*, and half of them became popular. The most popular was the plaintive "Crying for the Carolines." The jaunty "Have a Little Faith in Me" did particularly well with dance bands and singers, but the song that settled down to become a standard was a slightly sad love ballad, with a bit of basic wisdom in its opening Lewis and Young lines:

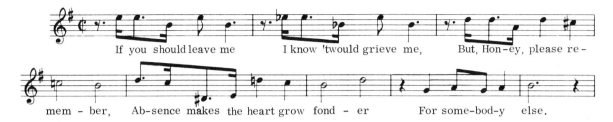

If you should leave me   I know 'twould grieve me,   But, Hon-ey, please re-

mem - ber,   Ab-sence makes the heart grow fond - er   For some-bod-y   else.

Harry Warren took no liking to California. A dyed-in-the-wool New Yorker, he missed the bustle of mid-Manhattan and the camaraderie of the music business, and he gladly returned. Neither did he care much for the film people and their attitude toward music. "I remember standing on the set and watching them do one of the numbers," he reminisces. "In those days they did everything directly for the cameras, with the orchestra right on the sound stage. I mentioned to the producer, Hal B. Wallis, that they were doing the lyrics wrong. He said, 'What's the difference? Who knows the right lyrics?' I pointed out that they were going to publish the songs, and the right lyrics would be available. This seemed to make no impression on him at all. Little did I realize that this would be typical of the attitude of movie producers toward music and that I would run into this sort of thing time and time again in the years to come."

Warren returned to his office at Remick in New York and continued to write songs with various lyricists. By now Billy Rose had worked himself up to a position of influence on Broadway, and he asked Warren if he would be interested in supplying a few songs for his upcoming revue, *Sweet and Low.* The show opened in November and contained three songs by Warren, two of them written with Mort Dixon and one with Ira Gershwin. The Warren-Gershwin song went:

There's a   cheer - ful   lit - tle   ear - ful,   Gosh,   I   miss   it   some - thing

fear - ful   And   this   cheer - ful   lit - tle   ear - ful   Is   the   well known "I   love   you."

Billy Rose insisted that his name be on the sheet music of all three songs, and although very little of the lyrics are his, Warren believes that Rose should be credited with the ideas for the songs and with some of the titles. The most durable song from *Sweet and Low* is "Would You Like to Take a Walk?" In the opinion of musicologist Alec Wilder, "The melody, verse and chorus, is very good writing, suggesting a wider knowledge of music than popular songs":

Mm - Mm - Mm   Would you   like   to take   a walk?   Mm - Mm - Mm   Do   you

think   it's gon - na rain?   Mm - Mm - Mm   How   a - bout   a sas - par - il - la?

Gee   the moon   is yel - ler   Sum - p'n good - 'll come   from   that

18

In March 1931 another Warren song appeared on Broadway when Al Jolson sang "Ma Mère" in *Wonder Bar*. Irving Caesar did the lyrics, with the egocentric Jolson insisting that he be listed as co-lyricist, since he had thought of the idea of the song. However, the sound of Jolson mooning about his mammy in French made no lasting impression.

The Warren song that caught the public fancy at this time was the somewhat ethereal ballad "By the River Sainte Marie," which he had written some years previously with Edgar Leslie. None of the publishers had felt that it was commercial, but by 1931, with a change of public mood from antic to subdued and an increasing value in Warren's name, Robbins, Feist and Miller Inc. took a chance on it:

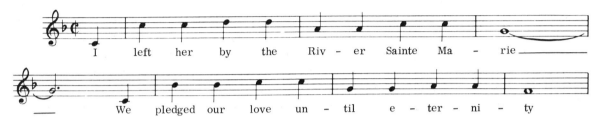

How the song came into being is an indication of Warren's character, revealing a gentle and sentimental streak perhaps not generally typical of commercial songwriters. "I went to see a movie called *The Enchanted Cottage*, and it was about a crippled boy and a crippled girl who loved each other. When they looked at one another they weren't crippled. This moved me so much that the melody of the song just came to me as I sat there looking at the picture."

Billy Rose staged another revue on Broadway, *Crazy Quilt*, which opened in May 1931 and

Another Vitagraph epic: Cameraman Arthur Quinn, assistant director Warren checking the script with director Walter Hall.

starred James Barton and Fannie Brice. Warren supplied four of the songs, one of them with Ira Gershwin, who was occasionally available when his brother George was writing music that didn't require lyrics. This was "In the Merry Month of Maybe," which gained some popularity, although nothing compared to the strength of "I Found a Million-Dollar Baby." Bing Crosby helped make the latter a national favorite, and it is now possible to look upon it as a uniquely American song, expressing a style and sentiment that could not have originated elsewhere. It also bears examination for its musical construction and its gentle cadences. Warren recalls, "It was Billy's idea. He had written a song with this title sometime before with another composer, but he didn't like it, so he gave his lyrics to Mort Dixon to rewrite and for me to come up with the melody."

Harry Warren's days as a song plugger were now far behind him, and he could spend his time in the manner he had long wanted—writing songs. The best of the lyricists were available and eager to work with him—Al Dubin, Gus Kahn, Ted Koehler, and Irving Kahal. Mort Dixon and Joe Young received an offer to write the lyrics to a new Ed Wynn show to be called *The Laugh Parade* and agreed with the producers that Warren was the man to write the music. This was his first complete Broadway score, but he was disappointed with it because the book was weak, the whole thing loosely structured around Ed Wynn, who ad-libbed and winged his way through the show. *The Laugh Parade* opened in November 1931 and pleased the crowds who came to be amused by the popular Wynn. Of the songs, only one emerged as a lasting winner. In fact, it can be said of "You're My Everything" that it is one of the mainstays in the art of the American song.

The call of Hollywood became stronger and stronger as one musical after another passed before the cameras. Warners delved into the catalog of Witmark, Harms and Remick for musical scores and requested the New York offices to get new songs from their contracted writers. Warren was offered trips to California to write for the movies but declined. Asked to write a song for *The Crooner*, which starred David Manners as a swelled-headed, megaphone-wielding singer—obviously a spoof on Rudy Vallee—Warren preferred to sit down in Manhattan with Irving Kahal to write *Three's a Crowd*. However, when Warners planned an expensive and original movie musical, to be called *42nd Street*, producer Darryl F. Zanuck requested Remick to send Warren to the coast. The challenge was too great to be passed up, and the somewhat hesitant Warren took the four-day train ride to Los Angeles. Of special interest to him was that Al Dubin would be the lyricist. Dubin had been at Warners for two years and had established himself with the success of "Tiptoe through the Tulips" and "Painting the Clouds with Sunshine," written with Joe Burke for *Gold Diggers of Broadway* in 1929.

Al Dubin was born in Zurich, Switzerland, in 1891 and brought to the United States at the age of two. He made his first attempts at songwriting while in school in Pennsburg, Pennsylvania, and in 1914 he moved to New York, where he found employment as a lyricist in Tin Pan Alley. He specialized in writing material for vaudevillians and enjoyed his first success in 1916, with " 'Twas Only an Irishman's Dream."

With U.S. entry into the war, Dubin joined the army and served in France with the 77th Division. Afterward he headed back to Manhattan to resume his struggle to make a living as a songwriter. Not until 1925 did he achieve recognition, when his song "A Cup of Coffee, a Sandwich and You," written with composer Joseph Meyer, was used in *Charlot's Revue*. Shortly after that he helped Sammy Fain write his first hit, "Nobody Knows What a Red-headed Woman Can Do," and teamed up with another young and budding composer, Jimmy McHugh, to write "My Dream of the Big Parade."

Dubin, like Warren, knew what it was like to spend years wondering if he would ever become a lasting success in the songwriting business. As Warren puts it, "I first met Al at the restaurant where so many of the songwriters gathered, Lindy's, and it was an appropriate place to meet him, because Al was a large man with an enormous appetite. He loved good food. Eating was an avocation with him, and he spent a lot of time seeking out restaurants. We hit it off immediately. The chemistry was right. Writing songs with a partner is like a marriage."

The main difference between Harry Warren and Al Dubin was one of attitude toward living in Los Angeles. Dubin took to it easily, and Warren didn't. "In the first place, it was nothing like it is today," says Warren. "The railway station was a wooden building, if you rented a car you were lucky if the wheels didn't fall off, and there were very few decent places to eat. Hollywood looked to me like a small town in South Dakota, and when you finally got to Warners studio in Burbank it was like being on an Indian outpost. You could look out across the San Fernando Valley, through the windows of the music department, and see nothing but empty land. Also, it was summer and hot as hell, and all I could think about was New York. What made it worse, the lot was almost empty—they had laid off most of their people. Warners had made a fortune with *The Jazz Singer*, but by the summer of 1932 they were in real trouble, and there was quite a bit of opposition in the company to making *42nd Street*."

1929 had brought droves of musical talent to Hollywood, all of them assuming they would do as well in the movies as they had on the stage. Time proved differently. Maurice Chevalier, Jeanette MacDonald, John Boles, and Eddie Cantor launched themselves successfully, but Sophie Tucker, Helen Morgan, Fannie Brice, and Ted Lewis did much less well. Poor George Jessel, who had turned down *The Jazz Singer* because the money wasn't big enough, tried to make amends with *Lucky Boy* and proved that as a movie star he was anything but.

All in all, about fifty musicals were made in Hollywood in 1929, and another one hundred films dragged in a song or two. The year produced quantity but not a great deal of quality, and by the end of the year some of the talent was buying itself tickets back to New York. The producers tried for a little better product in 1930. They brought in singers like Grace Moore, Lawrence Tibbett, John McCormick, and Dennis King, but none of them made a lasting impression. The public became tired of looking at photographed singers and dancers.

Fewer than twenty musicals were made in Hollywood in 1931, and it seemed that the musical was heading for a swift death. Only a dozen were made in 1932. Nonetheless, there were still a few people in the industry who believed that musicals would have a market if they were made in a more exciting way. Primitive recording techniques were a severe limitation, especially with camera movements curtailed because of microphones hanging from long-armed booms.

One of the few men who had the foresight to see that film musicals needed fluidity and a fusion of cinematic and musical techniques was Darryl F. Zanuck, then head of production for Warners. He had bought a property called *42nd Street*, and he persuaded Warners to put up some of their diminishing funds to produce it. Zanuck believed he had the performers he needed: the veteran Bebe Daniels and Warner Baxter, along with a pair of youngsters of great appeal—a handsome tenor named Dick Powell and Ruby Keeler, a pretty dancer who had the fortune to be Mrs. Al Jolson. In Warren and Dubin he knew he had the songwriters necessary for a good score, but what he badly needed was someone to stage the musical numbers in a way they had never been staged before. Discussing this with Mervyn LeRoy, Zanuck learned about Busby Berkeley, who had made a name for himself on Broadway as a choreographer with strikingly original ideas and who had just directed the musical sequences in an Eddie Cantor picture for Goldwyn.

42nd Street made all the difference. With its success, the movie musical moved to a new plateau of creativity. It became a distinctly American form of film, essentially a Hollywood product. Other people in other places sometimes made movie musicals, but the pattern was set and developed in California. Its lifespan was a full twenty years, from 1932 to 1952, and the composer who spent all those twenty years writing songs for the movies was Harry Warren.

21

I Found a Million Dollar Baby
(In a Five and Ten Cent Store)

Lyric by
BILLY ROSE and
MORT DIXON

Music by
HARRY WARREN

Diagrams for Guitar, Symbols for Ukulele and Banjo

You're My Everything

Words by
MORT DIXON
and JOE YOUNG

Music by
HARRY WARREN

*Diagrams for Guitar, Symbols for Ukulele and Banjo

PART TWO

THE YEARS WITH
THE
BROTHERS WARNER

Harry Warren and Al Dubin.

Come and meet____ those danc - ing feet,_____ On the Av - e - nue I'm tak -ing you to,___ For - ty Sec-ond Street.

The budget for *42nd Street* was set at four hundred thousand dollars, a large one for that time, particularly in view of Warners' lagging financial condition. It is doubtful whether the film would have materialized without the enthusiastic drive of Darryl F. Zanuck. His gamble paid off handsomely, and such was the zest and zip of the movie that it opened the door to a new concept in making movie musicals. Much of this was due to the appealingly bizarre and visually fascinating choreography of Busby Berkely, but it was also due to Lloyd Bacon's taut, upbeat direction.

42nd Street is the backstage, putting-on-a-show musical *par excellence*, and part of its success lies in the fact that Harry Warren and Al Dubin knew the territory very, very well. Perhaps because of this Zanuck decided to use them in the picture as the songwriters who rush up on the stage and accuse harried producer Warner Baxter of ruining their song. "The story called for a bad song," Warren says, "so we wrote a clinker and called it 'It Must Be June.' Baxter had to make a mess of it, and we had to protest, with him deciding to throw it out and tell us it stank. It's funny to watch the scene today. We look like a couple of gangsters."

33

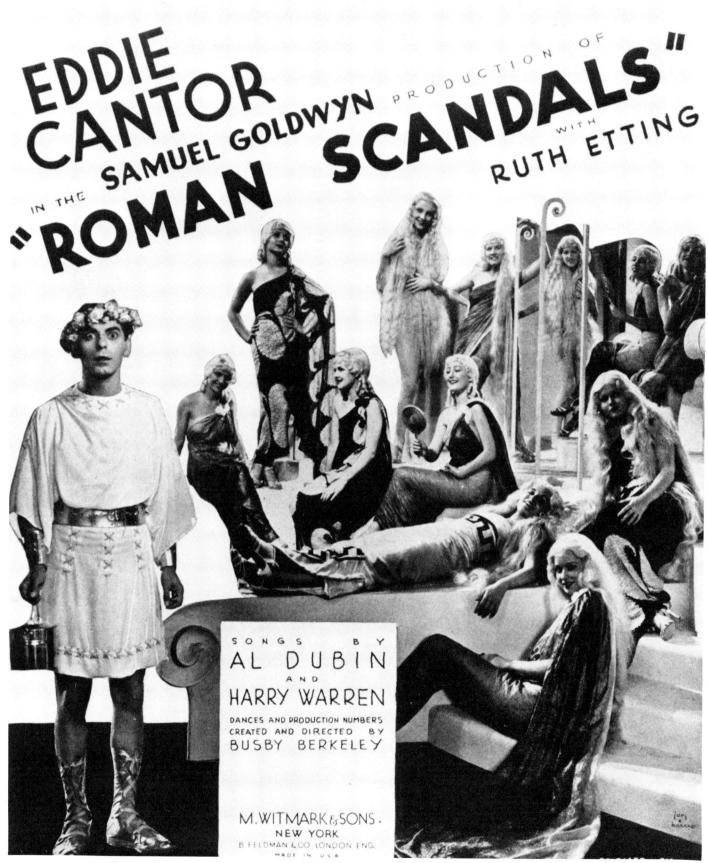

Roman Scandals

All four of the Warren-Dubin songs became popular, with "You're Getting to Be a Habit With Me" becoming a standard. In the picture it is sung by Bebe Daniels, as a Broadway star troubled by a slipping career and a mixed-up love life. Later she breaks an ankle and a young, inexperienced, wide-eyed innocent ("You're going out there a youngster but you've got to come back a star") takes her place and becomes a smash hit. Warren says that the song came out of a casual remark on the Warners lot. "Dubin liked to kid around with the girls. One of them was Leo Forbstein's secretary. She was going around with a certain fellow, and Dubin asked her why. She said, 'Oh, I don't know. He's getting to be a habit with me.' We used it right away."

Dick Powell had been signed by Warners a year previously, and they had used him in three small roles but he hit his stride in *42nd Street*, as did Ruby Keeler, who here made her movie debut after a few appearances on Broadway. She has always been among the first to admit that hers was a slim talent, but she caught the hearts of the Depression public and many years later proved that her special appeal still had a magic quality. Of the nine pictures she made at Warners, seven were with Dick Powell, making them one of the most popular teams of the thirties.

Powell would go on to star in thirty musicals for Warners, eighteen of them with music by Harry Warren. His big solo in *42nd Street* is "Young and Healthy," one of those optimistic ditties designed to boost the spirits of depressed Americans. In Berkeley's hands the song is a weird whirl of montage photography displaying a bevy of chorus girls and young Dick, who is bursting with good health. He was at this time twenty-eight but gave the impression of being younger, and his voice was still a tenor, sometimes a little strident, rather than the smooth, light baritone it would soon become.

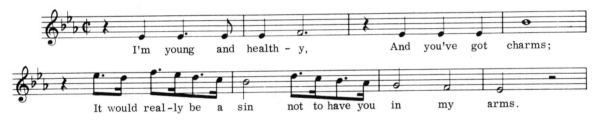

Berkeley's most impressive stunt in this picture is his staging of "Shuffle Off to Buffalo," in which he opens a Pullman railroad car like a jackknife and moves his camera down the aisle to peer—and leer—at the amorous young couples on their way to honeymoons at Niagara:

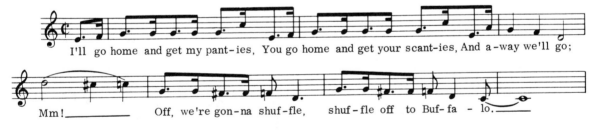

The finale of *42nd Street* is Berkeley's elaborate staging of the title song. Warren's staccato melody provides a perfect basis for tap dancing and rapidly switching camera angles. Ruby Keeler's dancing feet hammer out the message of jazzy night life in mid-Manhattan, and the chorus declaims "a rhapsody of laughter and tears" and the glory of the big parade that goes on for years. What looks like the skyline of New York bursts into squads of dancers, each manipulating a cardboard cutout of a skyscraper, and the number ends with a swift pan to the top of a building, where Dick and Ruby beam with satisfaction, as well they should. Audiences seeing the picture early in 1933 could hardly fail to be aware that this was a breakthrough in the presentation of song and dance on the screen.

42nd Street: the title song.

42nd Street: Una Merkel, Ruby Keeler and Ginger Rogers.

42nd Street: Warner Baxter rehearsing Dick Powell and Bebe Daniels.

42nd Street: The classic movie musical plot twist. Star Bebe Daniels sprains her foot, clearing the way for Ruby Keeler to take the spotlight. George Brent lends sympathy and Warner Baxter, as the director, starts to worry.

Powell and Keeler, Berkeley and Bacon, Warren and Dubin, all swept up by fate and thrown together in great success, almost as if in a Warner Bros. musical. The time, the talents, and the elements were in perfect harmony that could only lead to sequels. The only off-key note arising from all this was the public's strangely indifferent attitude toward the men who wrote the songs. Says Warren, "We were invited to the premiere at Grauman's Chinese Theatre, and we rented a car to take part in the parade. Kids would run up and look at us and turn away, saying, 'Oh, that's nobody.' That's about all we got at the premiere. The treatment at the studio wasn't much better. Music seems to be a mystery to those who are not involved in it, and they seem to have no idea how a composer works. It's a mystery to me that almost all the movie producers with whom I've worked have been musically ignorant people, even those who were making musicals, and they never seemed willing to give us the respect they would give to actors or technicians. I remember playing a waltz for one of the top producers at Warners. It was short and took only about a minute and a half to play. All he could say was, 'It couldn't have taken you very long to write that.'"

GOLD DIGGERS OF 1933

42nd Street had been completed by the end of 1932, but Warners delayed its release until the spring of 1933, realizing that they had a potential hit that would call for a sequel. However, as Harry Warren explains, "None of us thought that it would be *that* big and that it would start a whole cycle of these things." Warren had returned to his office at Remick in New York, with no interest in doing any more work for the movies. He hoped that his future would be with the Broadway theaters. Such was not to be. After writing the five songs for *Gold Diggers of 1933*, he and Dubin accepted a contract with Warners on a yearly renewable basis. From then on, like it or not, Harry Warren would be a composer of songs for the movies.

Gold Diggers of 1933 outdoes *42nd Street* in its production numbers. Busby Berkeley was clearly the man of the hour and was given an almost free hand in concocting his highly indivi- ual moments of choreography.

The picture opens with a flock of chorines led by Ginger Rogers, all dressed in tinsel cos- tumes and waving shields in the form of coins, singing, "We're in the Money." The song could hardly be more obviously a morale booster for Depression audiences, telling them 'The skies are sunny," and "We've got a lot of what it takes to get along," all to a bouncing Warren melody.

Like its predecessor, this picture also deals with the trials of putting on a stage show, with Dick Powell as a Bostonian blueblood yearning to be a songwriter but forbidden, on pain of disinheritance, to have anything to do with show business. His girlfriend, Ruby Keeler, is an unemployed showgirl, living with Joan Blondell and Aline McMahon, who are all hired by penniless producer Ned Sparks. Powell comes up with the money to produce the show, with the proviso that he cannot reveal his sources. This leads his associates to believe he might be a crook. Not that anyone cares where the money comes from, as long as they can get their show on the boards. It also gives Dick a chance to get his songs performed, and the first one he sings for producer Sparks is:

I've got to sing a torch song, For that's the way I feel; When I feel a thing, then I can sing, It must be real.

The show within the show allows for generous viewings of rehearsals, although there is no attempt to explain how these gargantuan Berkeley creations could possibly be staged in any theater. What Berkeley had struck upon was a new form of cinema, a visual fantasizing that recognized no boundaries, and in Warren and Dubin he had a composer and a lyricist fully capable of meeting the challenge.

Berkeley has received copious credit for his brilliant work, but it must be remembered that the songs came first and that in almost every instance the idea for the production began with Al Dubin. Says Warren, "Doing these pictures was very much like doing revues for the stage. You had to think all the time of material that could be performed for the camera and show the performers to advantage. We were called in to preproduction conferences, which was largely a waste of time because it was usually a discussion of costs, and the Warners executives were obsessed with economy. After that we would get a script, but there was seldom anything in it to suggest the songs, other than an indication of where they might go. For this one we knew we needed a song for the Gold Diggers, but there was nothing in the script about a Shadow Waltz or a Forgotten Man. Those were Dubin's ideas, and he deserves the credit for them."

The Gold Diggers of 1933: The chorus girls cheer up a depressed America with "We're in the Money." At $75 a week they were doing better than most.

The plot lines of *Gold Diggers of 1933* resolve themselves easily enough, with Powell overcoming his family's prejudice against show business, and his stiff-necked brother, Warren William, and the befuddled family lawyer, Guy Kibbee, ensnared by Blondell and McMahon. Of the five songs the most dated is "Pettin' in the Park," which wins attention mostly because of its sexual earthiness. The long sequence belabors the boy-after-girl gambit, with much display of skimpy lingerie and nude silhouettes, and ends rather libidinously with Powell using a can opener to cut Keeler out of her tin suit:

"Remember My Forgotten Man" is also dated, but such is its quality as both a song and a production number that it can be singled out as a particular highlight in the Warners musical cycle. In an otherwise lighthearted and pleasingly trivial film, this number provides dramatic validity and trenchant social commentary:

The song and its staging were a plea for the United States' vast army of unemployed, so many of whom were ex-servicemen reduced to standing in breadlines. The Warren melody lends itself both to the slow, incessant statement of the dramatic point of the song and to the martial beat for the soldiers. Joan Blondell, so often the comedienne at this point in her career, made the material particularly poignant.

The artistic highlight of *Gold Diggers 1933* is the lilting, swirling "Shadow Waltz." The Dubin lyrics are poetic, but hardly ever sung today. What survives is Warren's beautifully constructed waltz theme, a superior piece of composition that takes its place among the handful of great American waltzes. Berkeley put the music to striking and tasteful effect, with a group of girls waltzing while playing the violin. With a variety of camera angles, and cuts skillfully matching the rhythm, Berkeley whirls his girls to an engaging pattern of sight and sound, including blackout shots in which the violins are edged with neon lighting. Few sequences in movie musicals would ever equal the charm and grace of this beguiling "Shadow Waltz."

FOOTLIGHT PARADE (1933)

Warners' hurry to get another lavish musical on the screen resulted in *Footlight Parade*. The hurry is not apparent on the screen. In fact, in terms of its script it is a far better entry than

The Gold Diggers of 1933: Budding song writer Dick Powell sings "I've Got to Sing a Torch Song" for Broadway producer Ned Sparks, who thereupon pronounces Dick a genius and cries "Fire Dubin and Warren."

The Gold Diggers of 1933: Ruby Keeler, with blonde wig, leads her ensemble in playing "The Shadow Waltz."

The Gold Diggers of 1933: "The Shadow Waltz," a la Busby Berkeley.

either *42nd Street* or *Gold Diggers of 1933*. Admittedly, it is another backstage musical, but it is the best of them, with a feasible plot, tough and sometimes unflattering characterizations that reveal a lot about show business, and plenty of sharp and witty dialogue. Again the brisk direction is that of Lloyd Bacon, and again Busby Berkeley created some stunning sequences of screen choreography. However, the structure of the picture is odd in that the whole last half hour consists of three mammoth production numbers one after the other. Of these, two were written by Warren and Dubin, and the other, the celebrated "By a Waterfall," was written by Sammy Fain and Irving Kahal, who also supplied the picture with two other songs.

Footlight Parade is of historical interest since it deals with the long-defunct business of producing live-entertainment prologues to major film presentations. The picture opens with a producer of stage musicals, James Cagney, reacting with disgust to the news that sound movies have replaced the silents, the assumption being that this will kill off his kind of show. However, it dawns upon him that "mini" musicals presented as part of first-run-film shows might be a profitable new venture, and much of *Footlight Parade* deals with his efforts to make a success of it. The tough, harassed producer is beset with problems, such as a vicious wife, cheating employees, and a spy in the company who slips Cagney's ideas to the opposition. Cagney and his company gird their loins and confine themselves to their premises, with no one either coming in or going out, and then in one fantastic evening they race around New York in buses and stage their productions in three different theaters.

First comes "Honeymoon Hotel," which is something of an extension of "Shuffle Off to Buffalo" in its sexy display of young lovers with only love on their minds. The Berkeley staging is quite obvious, with Dick Powell and Ruby Keeler checking into a hotel where "every little bridal suite is heaven":

How a-bout a lit-tle cel-e-bra-tion, To the jin-gle of a wed-ding bell, How a-bout a lit-tle res-er-va-tion, At the Hon-ey-Moon Ho-tel.

The Gold Diggers of 1933: In staging "Pettin' in the Park" Berkeley revealed his odd mixture of elegance and vulgarity.

The Gold Diggers of 1933: Joan Blondell and dozens of male
extras performing "Remember My Forgotten Man."

Dubin's lyrics leave little doubt of intent: "Cupid is the night clerk,/'Neath the skies above:/He just loves his night work,/We just love to love." Despite much parading around in nightgowns and pajamas, the number is more innocuous than salacious, not on a par with the material that follows.

"By a Waterfall" is an elaborate and seemingly endless aquacade in which Berkeley exhausts the permutations of girlie patterns in fountains and swimming pools.

Of the three productions, the only one with a plot is "Shanghai Lil," in which producer Cagney has to perform himself when his leading man is incapable of going on. This was a blessing for the audience, because it gave Cagney a welcome opportunity to show his style as a dancer. Here he is a sailor on leave in Shanghai looking for a lost love:

I've cov-ered ev-'ry lit-tle high-way, And I've been climb-ing ev-'ry hill__

I've been look-in' high__ and I've been look-in' low,__ Look-in' for my Shang-hai Lil.___

Finally he finds her—Ruby Keeler with slanting eyes—and in their joy they hop up on a bar and tap-dance. But the navy bugle blows, and sailor Cagney and all the others form their ranks and march away to the docks, leaving poor Lil behind.

This impressive number gave Berkeley a chance to reveal his prowess with military drills, something he had mastered in the army in the First World War. Berkeley also showed his penchant for overhead shots, with the sailors making formations and designs to approximate the national emblem, the flag, and even a likeness of Franklin D. Roosevelt.

Harry Warren recalls, "About the only thing Dubin and I enjoyed at the preproduction meetings was watching Berkeley con the executives. He seldom had any idea what he was going to do until he got on a set, and mostly you would see him sitting there with his eyes half-closed, as in a trance. But at the meetings he would be required to explain what he wanted and how he was going to do it. He would give them long-winded explanations in double-talk that would confuse all of them. Their final question was always the same: 'How much is it going to cost?' He was the bane of the production chiefs. They would come onto his sets and see a hundred girls sitting around doing their knitting while he thought up his ideas. They just couldn't figure him out. Neither could we much of the time. We used to call Buzz 'The Madman.' "

ROMAN SCANDALS (1933)

After completing the music for *Gold Diggers of 1933*, Harry Warren returned to New York, still a nonconvert to California and still hoping he could continue to live on Long Island. He received a call to join Eddie Cantor at his hotel to discuss a movie project. Al Dubin also happened to be in New York, and Cantor asked them if they would interested in writing the songs for his next film for Samuel Goldwyn. Cantor wanted to do something with an Ancient Roman setting, and the title, *Roman Scandals*, came out of the conference. Warren believes it was most likely Dubin's idea. In accepting the job the pair were once again united with Busby Berkeley, who had committed himself to Goldwyn before signing his Warners contract. It was Goldwyn who had first brought Berkeley to Hollywood, to do Eddie Cantor's *Whoopee*, but in order to get Berkeley for *Roman Scandals* Goldwyn had to take legal action against Warners.

Of the five songs, three are memorable, although only one, "Keep Young and Beautiful,"

Footlight Parade

Most of the time Harry Warren and Al Dubin got along smoothly.

. . . but sometimes Dubin took a disliking to the music . . .

47

has maintained an identity. Most of the film is set in Imperial Rome, but it opens in a small Oklahoma town called West Rome, where Cantor is a genial, wistful loner who studies Roman history and stumbles upon corruption in the town. He sides with a group of poor townspeople who are being evicted from their homes for failure to meet their mortgages, and he brightens their spirits with a cheery song about life in the open air:

With a mil-lion lit-tle stars,_____ We can dec-o-rate the ceil-ing,___

___ With an op-ti-mis-tic feel-ing_____ We can build a lit-tle home.

Evicted from the town, Cantor trudges along the highway and daydreams about Rome. The scene dissolves, and next we see him being picked up by a group of Roman soldiers, who turn him over to slave auctioneers. Because of his strange and amusing personality he escapes torture and gets assigned to the home of the emperor, Edward Arnold, as a food taster. He also makes the acquaintance of a deposed courtesan, played by the greatly popular singer Ruth Etting. In her despair she sings "No More Love," a song of minor modes and almost operatic construction:

No more sun,_____ In the sky a-bove, Clouds are all I

see, There's no more love,_____ in your heart for me.

Etting's performance of the song is poignant, and skillfully backed by Alfred Newman's conducting of Ray Heindorf's orchestral and choral arrangement. The singing is followed by a Berkeley ballet of marked eroticism, with sensuous, scantily clad slave girls mistreated by guards, and a final wail from Etting, "There's no more love in your heart for me."

The musical highlight of *Roman Scandals* comes when Cantor, trying to escape the palace guards, wanders into the quarters of the emperor's ladies, a harem of splendid proportions. To this beautiful group, The Goldwyn Girls, Cantor delivers a sprightly song of advice:

Keep young and beau-ti-ful,__ It's your du-ty to be beau-ti-ful__

Keep young and beau-ti-ful__ If you want to be loved

In the course of his Roman adventures Cantor halts the comedy to sing "Rome Wasn't Built in a Day," and to the emperor he suggests, "Put a Tax on Love." Eventually he makes his escape from Rome in a wild chariot chase, and after getting knocked out, he awakens to find himself back in West Rome.

By now the corrupt officials have been exposed, and Eddie is hailed as the hero of the townspeople, whom he joins in singing and dancing to the happy strains of "Build a Little Home." *Roman Scandals* is, perhaps, the best of Cantor's movies, and Harry Warren claims, "Eddie was a very nice man. He was kind and considerate when a great many people in this business weren't."

Roman Scandals: Al Dubin and Harry Warren on the set at the Goldwyn Studio at the filming of their "Keep Young and Beautiful."

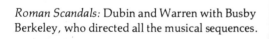

Roman Scandals: Dubin and Warren with Busby Berkeley, who directed all the musical sequences.

Roman Scandals: Some of the reasons why the song writers spent a lot of time hanging around the sets.

Warren also speaks highly of Samuel Goldwyn. "Aside from being very shrewd, he was a man with great taste, and he didn't mind spending money, which was the opposite of the situation at Warners. But I think he resented the gouging he got from Warners in order to use Berkeley. I don't know what we cost Goldwyn, but I imagine Warners was relieved to have us off salary for a while. And, of course, they published all the music we did for *Roman Scandals*.

"Goldwyn was very much interested in what Berkeley was doing and came to a lot of the rehearsals, but he was one man Buzz couldn't con with his double-talk. We also had Ruth

After completing *Footlight Parade*, Harry Warren went to New York, where Warners produced a short feature devoted to his music for their pictures. That's Harry at the piano.

Etting's husband, Marty, around all the time—'the Gimp' as he was called. He was a rough, crude character, a former Chicago racketeer, and he would slap Goldwyn on the back and hug him. This confused Goldwyn, who was dignified, not the kind you slapped on the back. Dubin confused him too. Goldwyn always called him 'Dugan,' and since Al was mostly off the lot, probably cruising around looking for restaurants, I was always being asked, 'Where's Dugan?' Goldwyn wanted to hire us for another picture, but it never came to be."

MOULIN ROUGE (1934)

Darryl F. Zanuck resigned as head of production for Warners in 1933, partly because he felt constricted but mostly because he wanted his own production company. Since he was a hot young producer, the field was open to him, but he chose to go with Twentieth Century, this being a year before their merger with the Fox Corporation. In his first year Zanuck supervised the production of a dozen pictures, among them *Moulin Rouge*, a romantic musical designed as a vehicle for top star Constance Bennett. The picture was filmed at the Goldwyn studio and released by United Artists.

Moulin Rouge came on the heels of the Cantor picture, and Warren and Dubin were beginning to feel that their future with Warners might be one of loanouts. However, this was the last time it was to happen, and once they returned to the Burbank lot Warners kept them constantly busy. As Warren puts it, "People often ask me if I have a 'trunk,' that traditional box songwriters are supposed to use for their rejected songs. The answer is no. Dubin and I were so busy that we didn't have time to write anything other than the songs we had to do for the pictures—and almost every song was used. For me it was the same at the other studios."

Moulin Rouge is yet another backstage musical, no more probable than the others. Here Constance Bennett plays dual roles, as a pair of twin sisters who are entertainers. One of them marries a songwriter, Franchot Tone, who doesn't want his wife to continue her career, and the other goes off to Paris, where she becomes famous under a foreign name. The first sister separates from her husband, and he hires the foreign star for his Broadway show, not knowing her true identity. When she arrives in New York she sympathizes with the sister, who still loves her husband, and lets her take over the role. Then, in the guise of the foreign star, the wife flirts with her own husband and manages to rekindle his love.

Of the three Warren-Dubin songs, the one heard most in the film, both sung and used thematically, is "The Song of Surrender," but it made no lasting impression. Constance Bennett performed her own singing, but the film also used the voices of the Boswell Sisters and crooner Russ Colombo, whose life was to end a few months later in an accident. His singing of "Coffee in the Morning, Kisses in the Night" helped that song find favor with the public.

I've got a mis-sion, it's just a sim-ple thing I've on-ly one am-bi-tion, To have the right to bring you your cof-fee in the morn-ing and kiss-es in the night.____

The hit song of *Moulin Rouge* turned out to be the rather somber "The Boulevard of Broken Dreams," which appears in the picture as a production number by the "foreign star" at a theater in Paris. The Dubin lyrics tell a sad tale, and the Warren melody has the sultry quality of a French-apache dance. An unlikely hit, it was to become a classic torch song:

I walk a - long the street of sor - row ___ the Bou - le-vard of Bro -ken Dreams ___ Where Gig - o -lo ___ and Gig - o - lette, ___ can take a kiss ___ with- out re - gret. ___ So they for-get their bro - ken dreams

Warren spoke highly of working for Zanuck: "He was unlike some of the producers I've suffered under. If you played a piece they didn't like, they would say something like 'No good; get something else.' Zanuck was polite and sympathetic. If he didn't care for a melody he would say, 'Let's put that one away for a while and perhaps use it elsewhere. Do you have anything else?' Perhaps it was because he had been a writer, but he was interested in what we were doing—in fact, he was interested in every phase of production, which is what made him a first-class producer. He was a martinet, and it was amusing to see him parading around with his squad of 'yes men,' but nobody could say he didn't know his business."

Moulin Rouge: Tullio Carminati hangs on to Franchot Tone, as a Broadway composer-director, as he reaches out to his "French" star—Constance Bennett in a dark wig.

WONDER BAR (1934)

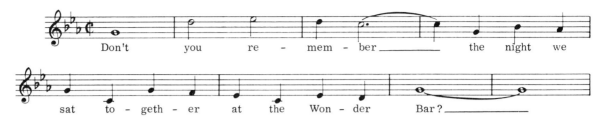

Don't you re - mem - ber _____ the night we
sat to - geth - er at the Won - der Bar? _____

For *Wonder Bar*, Harry Warren and Al Dubin were once again teamed with Lloyd Bacon and Busby Berkeley, expected to come up with more delights for the ear and the eye. *Wonder Bar* may not be the best remembered of the Warner musicals, but it is probably the one with the best screenplay (by Earl Baldwin, based on a German play), and it has moments of drama and tragedy to go along with the songs and the comedy. Al Jolson had appeared in the Broadway show of the same name, but none of the Broadway music was used in the picture.

Almost all the film takes places in a nightclub operated by a slick entertainer named Al Wonder, who occasionally regales his customers with a snappy song like "Vive La France" and an elaborate production number like "Goin' to Heaven on a Mule." His singing band leader, also a songwriter, is Dick Powell, who is in love with dancer Dolores Del Rio, but she loves her partner, Ricardo Cortez, a charming rogue who rejects her affections and makes a play for wealthy but unhappily married Kay Francis. Cortez winds up dead, having been stabbed by the jealous Del Rio, but the magnanimous Al covers up the crime, and she takes to the arms of Powell.

Musically, *Wonder Bar* is exceptionally well scored, and although none of the six compositions were to become lasting favorites, their quality is high and they are well integrated with the rather complicated plot lines. The film contains one of Warren's few instrumental pieces, the "Tango Del Rio," written for a dance sequence between Del Rio and Cortez. And the love-sick Powell sits at a piano and sings to the beautiful Dolores something he has written especially for her:

I see some-bod - y just like you,__ Pre-par -ing break-fast just for two,__
A dream that nev - er does come true,__ Why do I dream those dreams?

Wonder Bar's most impressive footage consists of Berkeley's staging of "Don't Say Good-night," a beguiling waltz song in which a large group of ballroom dancers were photographed, incredibly, within an octagon of huge mirrors:

When this love-ly dance is o - ver____ Don't say,__ "Good - night,"____
Let me live this mo- ment o - ver,_____ Don't say,___ "Good - night."

Since *Wonder Bar* starred the egocentric Al Jolson, it was mandatory to compose at least one special production number for him. Since he was renowned for appearing in blackface, it was decided to do a story about an old black man who dies and goes to heaven, taking his mule with him. Warren had completely written the jaunty melody, which inspired Dubin to come up with the concept of the material. It appealed to Jolson and Berkeley, alllowing both of them plenty of scope for old-fashioned minstrel-type entertainment and a distinctly *kitsch* depiction of a black heaven, full of little pickaninnies and lovable caricatures. The sequence, which seems ludicrous today, is particularly offensive to black Americans. "Goin' to Heaven on a Mule" is a glaring example of racial attitudes of 1934:

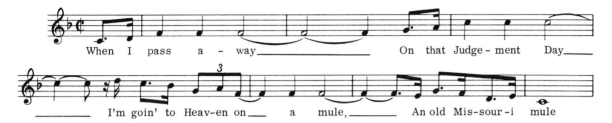

About Al Jolson, Warren says, "It wasn't a problem to write for him. He always like what we did and never offered any criticism, but he was dying to get his name on the sheet music. He asked if he could write a verse or two. He'd done this with other songwriters, but Dubin and I were determined his name wouldn't be on ours. It was great to have Jolson do your songs—he really knew how to put them over—but he liked people to think they were all his."

TWENTY MILLION SWEETHEARTS (1934)

Most of the songs Dick Powell sang in his first two years at Warners were those of Warren and Dubin, and plenty more were to come. Powell had become a great favorite with moviegoers by this time, with a steady stream of recordings and radio appearances backing up his pictures. Says Warren, "Of all the singers I've ever dealt with, he was just about the easiest to get along with. I don't think he ever made an objection to any song we handed him. Music was easy for him—he'd been a musician, and he'd been singing since he was a choirboy. His only problem at Warners was getting more money. Even when he was doing *42nd Street* he was only getting $175 a week, and it was a constant fight to raise it."

Moulin Rouge: Part of the elaborate "Boulevard of Broken Dreams" sequence.

The stars of *Wonder Bar*: Dick Powell, Ricardo Cortez, Dolores Del Rio and Al Jolson, looking as if he has a severe case of heartburn.

Wonder Bar: Dick Powell croons his love to Dolores Del Rio with "Why Do I Dream Those Dreams?"

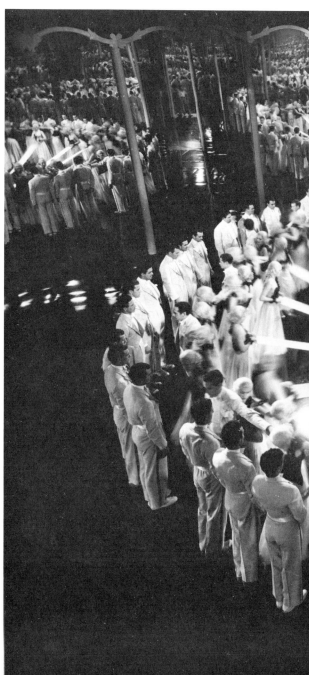

Al Jolson rehearsing *Wonder Bar* with his accompanist Martin Fried, to the apparent satisfaction of Warren and Dubin.

Wonder Bar: Busby Berkeley's lavish treatment of "Don't Say Goodnight" using a huge octagon of mirrors.

Twenty Million Sweethearts was Powell's eighth film as a star, and in this he co-starred with Ginger Rogers, who by now had made her first picture with Fred Astaire, *Flying Down to Rio.* The plot is as light as air, with Powell as a singing waiter picked up by a brash agent, Pat O'Brien, whose wild publicity schemes prove ever embarrassing to the mild crooner. O'Brien gets him into radio, but he is afraid of microphones, and it takes the kindness of another singer, Ginger, to settle him down to fame on the airwaves. She has lost her own show, but love brings success for them both.

Of the four songs, the perky "Out for No Good" and the sly ballad "What Are Your Intentions?" were only of fleeting interest. Much more substantial was "Fair and Warmer," a song with an optimistic point of view and a jazzy beat:

It's get-ting fair and warm-er,_____ Just be-cause you're in my arms,__ my dear.

In the film Powell sings the song with the Mills Brothers, doing some of the "scat" singing that was popular in 1934. The orchestra in the film is that of Ted Fiorito, and Powell afterward recorded the song with them. But the enduring hit from *Twenty Million Sweethearts* is a love song, a major item in the Warren catalog:

You may not be an an-gel, 'Cause an-gels are so few,

But un-til the day that one comes a-long, I'll string a-long with you.

The song once again reveals Warren's predilection for the lyrical flow of the Puccini school of opera. As for the inspiration, he says, "It was another of those casual remarks that Dubin picked up. I think he heard it in a movie, and once he had the first couple of lines of the lyric I was able to do the whole melody. This was an easy one."

Warren's chief recollection of *Twenty Million Sweethearts* concerns a scene in which Powell, at a broadcast, is singing "I'll String Along with You." The scene called for him to be nervous and to become so hoarse that he couldn't continue and for Ginger Rogers to take over. "They were recording the song," Warren says, "and Ginger couldn't hit the cue, the point at which she was supposed to pick up the song. After twenty-four takes I couldn't stand it any more and left."

Leo Forbstein, the head of the Warner music department, made his only screen appearance in this picture. "Leo did most of the conducting in the early thirties," Warren says, "but he gradually phased himself out because the job of running the department became too big. He really wasn't a very good conductor, but he was a great administrator and a very sympathetic man. Warners gave him complete authority and a big budget, and he made that department just about the best in the industry. He hired all the best men for the orchestra and treated them well, and it was Leo who brought in Steiner and Korngold. There were a lot of things I didn't like about working at Warners, but that music department, that was a gem."

On the set of *Wonder Bar:* Al Jolson threatens columnist
Sidney Skolsky as Busby Berkeley, Harry Warren and
producer Charles Einfeldt look on.

DAMES (1934)

What do you go for, Go see a show for? Tell the truth, you go to see those beau-ti-ful dames.

Dames differed so little from the previous Berkeley musicals that only an expert can separate it from the others. Again Dick Powell is a songwriter with a show that needs a backer, Ruby Keeler the inspiring girlfriend, and Joan Blondell the good chum showgirl who snares Guy Kibbee into putting up the money. The title song—Warren claims that he and Dubin tried to come up with a song in every picture that more or less summed up the whole thing—serves a good purpose for Berkeley to launch into another of his complicated, fanciful routines involving geometically displayed girls. Powell begins the song in his office, telling a group of would-be backers that pretty girls are what the business is all about, and as a string of lovelies passes through his office he warmly greets them, including "Miss Warren" and "Miss Dubin." After Powell's exposition of the song Berkeley takes over, and for the next five or six minutes the screen moves into his netherworld of cinema surrealism.

Less fantastic is "The Girl at the Ironing Board," with Joan Blondell as a love-sick young laundress yearning for the men who fill the shirts and underwear she irons. The song is deliberately old-fashioned, with a Gay Nineties lilt to it, and Blondell, no singer to speak of, used her own voice throughout. Berkeley's tricks are limited to having the clothes respond with gestures and dances to Joan's serenading. This was accomplished by having an army of men overhead manipulating strings. The song was not intended for the Hit Parade, but it has an appealing quality, amusingly performed by Blondell.

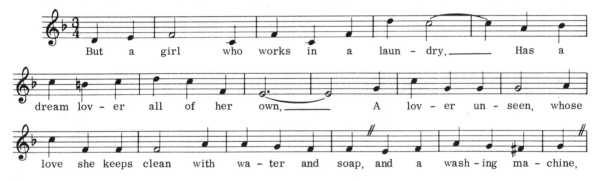

But a girl who works in a laun - dry,_____ Has a dream lov - er all of her own,_____ A lov - er un - seen, whose love she keeps clean with wa - ter and soap, and a wash - ing ma - chine,

Wonder Bar: Al Jolson singing "Goin' to Heaven on a Mule." In 1934 the orchestra was still being recorded on the set with the singers. Leo Forbstein is conducting and Harry Warren is the second figure to the right, wearing a fedora.

20 Million Sweethearts: Leo Forbstein, the head of Warners' music department, conducts the band for Dick Powell.

60

20 Million Sweethearts: Filming Dick Powell singing "I'll String Along With You" with Ted Fiorito and his Orchestra in the background.

20 Million Sweethearts: Dick Powell and Ginger Rogers.

61

Dames included several other songs by Sammy Fain and Irving Kahal, and Mort Dixon and Allie Wrubel, but Berkeley chose not to use any of their material for his sequences. Since the other writers had long been friends of Warren's, he didn't have to explain that the choice was not his. However, this would cause some embarrassment for him as time went by.

This film has the distinction of being the birthplace of "I Only Have Eyes for You," one of Warren's finest melodies and, as Alec Wilder says in his book *American Popular Song* (Oxford University Press, 1972): "It's a very lovely melody, beautifully and dramatically fashioned. It is another of those songs that needs no harmony in order to please."

However, for Busby Berkeley it was a diving board into yet another fantasy. It begins with Powell singing to Keeler on the Staten Island ferry, and then they fall asleep on the New York subway, triggering a dream sequence that has Ruby's face reproduced a hundredfold, thanks to Benda masks. Platoons of girls looking like Ruby waltz to the melody, and in one intricate exercise they form a group and bend over, with the boards on their backs making a gigantic jigsaw picture of Ruby's face.

This delighted the moviegoers, but Warren found it all a bit wearisome. "On screen they go through the song about twenty-five times," he says, "but on the set and at the recording session it seemed like nine thousand. Buzz never knew when to quit. I got sick of hearing the melody and began to hate it. Warners had given it a lot of promotion before the picture came out, so that it was already a hit. But once the movie was out it stopped selling. I guess the public felt saturated, the way I did."

SWEET MUSIC (1935)

Rudy Vallee was never quite able to duplicate in the movies the vast success he enjoyed on radio and with recordings. He had made a disastrous movie debut in 1929 with *The Vagabond Lover* and let six years go by before he made another stab at Hollywood. The result was *Sweet Music*, in which Vallee appears as a singing band leader working his way to success in New York and feuding with a song-and-dance girlfriend, Ann Dvorak. The picture did only mild business, and of the half dozen songs required Warren and Dubin supplied only the title number:

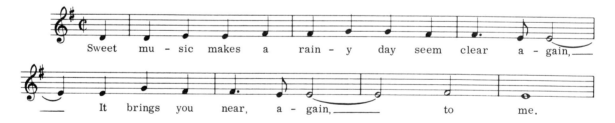

Sweet mu - sic makes a rain - y day seem clear a - gain,___ ___ It brings you near, a - gain,___ ___ to me.

The song was written to fit Vallee's limited crooning, and he recorded it, but it never gained much popularity.

Warren's next assignment was to write a title song for the Kay Francis soap opera *Living on Velvet*, but it was hardly worth the effort. The picture was mediocre, and even Dubin's inventiveness couldn't be very convincing about the joy of living on velvet.

GOLD DIGGERS OF 1935

Busby Berkeley had been nagging Warners to let him completely direct one of their musicals —not just the dance sequences, but the entire film. With *Gold Diggers of 1935* he got his wish.

On the set of *20 Million Sweethearts:* Harry Warren is to the right of Dick Powell, with Ginger Rogers behind them and director Ray Enright to the left. Pat O'Brien peers from the back while Leo Forbstein looms in the foreground. To the left of Forbstein is ace cameraman George Barnes.

Its distinction is that it contains "The Lullaby of Broadway," which brought Warren and Dubin their first Oscar and gave Berkeley the basis for his finest piece of work on the screen. As a film it is somewhat below the standard set by the others, with Dick Powell taking solo billing for the first time, paired with the not very exciting Gloria Stuart. She was billed below even Adolphe Menjou.

The story is set in a swank summer hotel in the country and opens with the staff sprucing up the place in preparation for the arrival of rich guests. Powell is a desk clerk, and Gloria is the daughter of millionairess Alice Brady. The device used to stage the lavish production numbers is a slight one—Brady is in the habit of staging an annual charity show at the hotel, and this time she is bamboozled into hiring an eccentric Russian producer, Menjou, who is in league with the hotel to chisel as much money as they can from her. Despite these venal attitudes and the usual obstacle course of comic mishaps, Menjou manages to mount a pair of magnificent production numbers of the kind that couldn't be staged anywhere except on a huge movie set.

Of the three songs in the picture the most modestly staged is "I'm Going Shopping with You," as penniless Powell accompanies spendthrift Gloria Stuart on a shopping binge in a big department store:

Berkeley's treatment of "The Words in My Heart" is yet another of his better productions and done with good taste. Warren's melody is a waltz in the best Viennese style, with hesitation beats, and Dubin's lyrics are very sentimental. In this instance the music is very much a part of the man. "I love to write waltzes more than any other kind of melody," Warren says. Following the statement of the song by Powell, made up as a costumed gentleman, Berkeley uses the music as a ballet for fifty white-clad girls playing fifty white baby-grand pianos. Unseen, almost, are fifty men in black under the piano shells, following marks on the black floor. What must have sounded improbable at the production conference actually comes off with genuine style, wafted along on a beguiling melody:

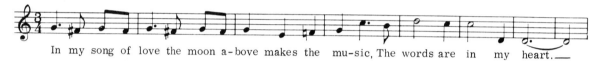

"The Lullaby of Broadway" is a film within a film. Its story is about a girl, Wini Shaw, who sleeps by day and lives a giddy life at night. The photography is exceptionally good—by George Barnes, who worked on many of these pictures—and the sequence never stops moving. Its highlight takes place in a nightclub in which Wini and Powell appear to be the only customers. A pair of Latin dancers glide through the dance and then lead what becomes almost a tidal wave of tap dancers, photographed from every conceivable angle. The sound of their thunderous tapping had to be recorded separately, to avoid blotting out the orchestra.

Harry Warren wrote the melody of "The Lullaby of Broadway" in its entirety ahead of the lyrics and with no direct inspiration. Its construction was different from the usual film song, running longer and containing no verse. He played the piece for Al Dubin and gave him a lead sheet. Dubin then disappeared, as was his wont, and several days later telephoned and invited Warren to his beach house.

As Warren tells it, "Al and I were always arguing about the relative merits of New York and Hollywood. I still hated it out here and talked all the time about New York, whereas he enjoyed the California life. When I got to his place he told me that he had written a lyric especially for me, a song in praise of New York.

"It was obviously a great piece of material, and I played it as soon as I could for Berkeley and for Jack Warner. Berkeley liked it, but he wasn't immediately enthusiastic about it. Warner didn't care much for it and shook his head and said, 'Tell Al to write a new lyric.'

"At this I got very brave and replied, 'I'll write you a new song, but I won't divorce this lyric from this melody,' and left.

"We were at this time also working on *Go into Your Dance* with Al Jolson. I played it for him, and even before I finished he was hopping around, saying that he had to have it. He ran to Warner's office and demanded, 'I gotta have that song in my picture.' Warner shrugged and agreed.

Dames: Part of Busby Berkeley's long routine for "I Only Have Eyes For You" involved having all the girls look like Ruby Keeler. The real Ruby is the one standing on the steps.

Dames:
More Ruby Keeler
look-alike-ism.

"Soon after that Berkeley, who hadn't even thought of using the song, heard what Jolson had done, and now he ran to Warner's office and protested that we had written the song for his picture. He put up such a stink that Warner had to let him have it. But it might never have been used as it was if it hadn't been for Jolson's enthusiasm. A lot of negative things can be said about Jolie, but he was an instinctive showman."

GO INTO YOUR DANCE (1935)

If you've been sing-in' a sad and blue__ song, Go in-to your dance.__

Go into Your Dance was filmed at the same time as *Gold Diggers of 1935*, with Bobby Connolly as the choreographer and Archie Mayo as the director. The picture was rushed into production to capitalize on Al Jolson's finally making a film with his wife, Ruby Keeler. Jolson needed success the way a diabetic needs insulin, and yet with the public clamoring for a sequel he refused because he feared they wanted him and Ruby as a team and not him for himself. Such was Jolson's all-consuming ego.

With both Berkeley and Jolson demanding their services, Warren and Dubin were under a strain. "We were asked to have lunch with Jack Warner in the executive dining room," Warren says. "That was a bad sign. Whenever the bosses call you in for lunch and tell you you're 'one of the family' and how they appreciate your work, you can guess they're in trouble. According to our contract we didn't have to work on two pictures at the same time, but neither Al nor myself could see any way of refusing. We got annoyed only when as we were looking at a work print of the picture in a projection room, and when the lights went up Jack Warner was surprised we were there. He told us we had been laid off. Our contract called for forty weeks a year, but they could exercise the twelve weeks of lay-off at their convenience, which they sometimes did without bothering to let us know. At times like that we didn't quite feel we were 'one of the family.' "

Of the seven songs for *Go into Your Dance*, two were to become great favorites and forever associated with Jolson—"About a Quarter to Nine" and "A Latin from Manhattan," both featuring dancing by Ruby. The first is a paean from Jolson to the girl he loves. The second is a more lavish number about a dancing girl who tries to pass herself off as a sensation from South America, Ruby as Señorita Donnalu, but is amiably spotted as a fraud by Jolson.

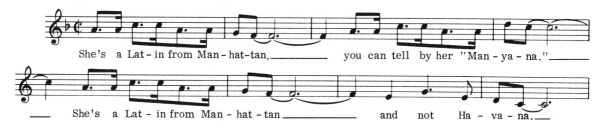

She's a Lat-in from Man-hat-tan,_____ you can tell by her "Man-ya-na."__

__ She's a Lat-in from Man-hat-tan_____ and not Ha-va-na.__

Go into Your Dance is a fast-paced ninety minutes of backstage hokum, extending itself a little beyond the norm to take in a murder mystery. Jolson struts as a happy-go-lucky, irresponsible entertainer who finally gets suspended by Actors Equity for missing one show too many. This doesn't seem to bother him, and he continues to spend his money at the racetracks. The murder of a fellow entertainer puts him in a bad light, but the strength of his sister, Glenda Farrell, and the love of Ruby pulls him through, and changes his ways.

Jolson sings all through the picture. He belts out a snappy song in praise of the place where he works, "The Casino De Paree," and sings about the fun of "A Good Old-Fashioned Cocktail with a Good Old-Fashioned Girl," a tuneful song but not destined to have any lasting meaning. The title song is, of course, self-explanatory and provides an opportunity for some spirited obvious but charming lyric, with a flowing lilt from Warren. Unfortunately, the song was so clearly Jolson material that it never received the attention from other singers it deserved:

Let oth-ers sing a - bout the moon,— as long as I — can croon a tune,— Oh! Mam - my,——— I'll sing a - bout you.

Go into Your Dance was also one of the last films in which Helen Morgan appeared. The celebrated torch singer with the small, wistful voice had made a number of films, but with nothing like the impact of her live work in New York nightclubs and theaters. Her personal life was blighted with unrequited love affairs and alcoholism. For her particular style Warren and Dubin wrote this minor-mode ballad:

Those ash-es on the floor,— the way you'd slam the door;— I miss them when the day is thru,— When I sit a-lone and think of you — and the lit-tle things you used to do.—

Also sad was Jolson's compulsive ego. His screen career had been floundering, but he might have prolonged his Hollywood career if he had agreed to make another picture with Ruby. With Jolson, though, it was a matter of solo spotlight or none at all. "It was great to have Jolson sing our songs," says Warren, "but he never wanted to have to say who wrote them. People would ask him, and he'd reply with a raised eyebrow and say, 'Who wrote them?' as if

Dames: At the conclusion of Berkeley's treatment of "I Only Have Eyes For You" the camera closes on a sleeping Ruby and Dick, probably lulled, in Harry Warren's opinion, by the seemingly endless repeats of the melody over the previous ten minutes.

the question shouldn't have been asked. Georgie Jessel summed him up beautifully when he said, 'He was a son of a bitch, but he was the greatest entertainer there ever was.' "

IN CALIENTE (1935)

Busby Berkeley and director Lloyd Bacon were turned loose on *In Caliente*, with Dolores Del Rio taking top billing as a dancer and Pat O'Brien as the newspaperman who at first criticizes her and then falls in love with her. None of them were able to breathe much life into it. The songwriting assignment was handed to Mort Dixon and Allie Wrubel, who came up with a hit in "The Lady in Red," sung by Wini Shaw. But again Berkeley insisted that Warners instruct Warren and Dubin to write a song for which he could dream up something fanciful.

"Muchacha" was not destined to become a hit, but it inspired Berkeley to build a huge set in the form of a Mexican bandits' cave hideaway, complete with dancing, brawling, a campfire, Phil Regan as a singing *bandido*, and eight white horses. Recalls Warren, "It was awful. The horses were nervous and panicked, they relieved themselves all over the place, they bolted off the set and people had to jump clear of them. And through it all was poor Phil Regan trying to act nonchalant, singing his song of amorous conquest":

BROADWAY GONDOLIER (1935)

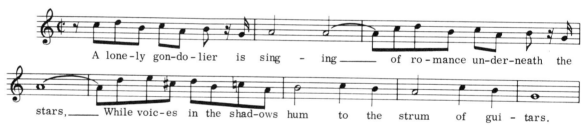

Broadway Gondolier was designed strictly as a Dick Powell vehicle to please those who enjoyed his singing—and by this time anyone with a radio had a hard time avoiding Powell's singing. Directed by workhorse Lloyd Bacon, with little in the way of production values, the film has Powell as a New York taxi driver who wants to make a living as a singer in radio but can't get the necessary break. However, his girlfriend, Joan Blondell—who was shortly to become Mrs. Dick Powell in reality—happens to be the secretary of radio executive Grant Mitchell. Mitchell's wife, Louise Fazenda, is a busybody who foists her tastes off on her husband, and she has a soft spot for tenors, especially when they sing of love:

Ann Dvorak and Rudy Vallee in *Sweet Music.*

On the set of *Sweet Music:* Harry
Warren plays for Ann Dvorak.

The Gold Diggers of 1935: The fifty pianos that waltzed to "The Words Are in My Heart." The actual waltzing was done by men in black suits following markings on the black floor, guiding the lightly built piano frames.

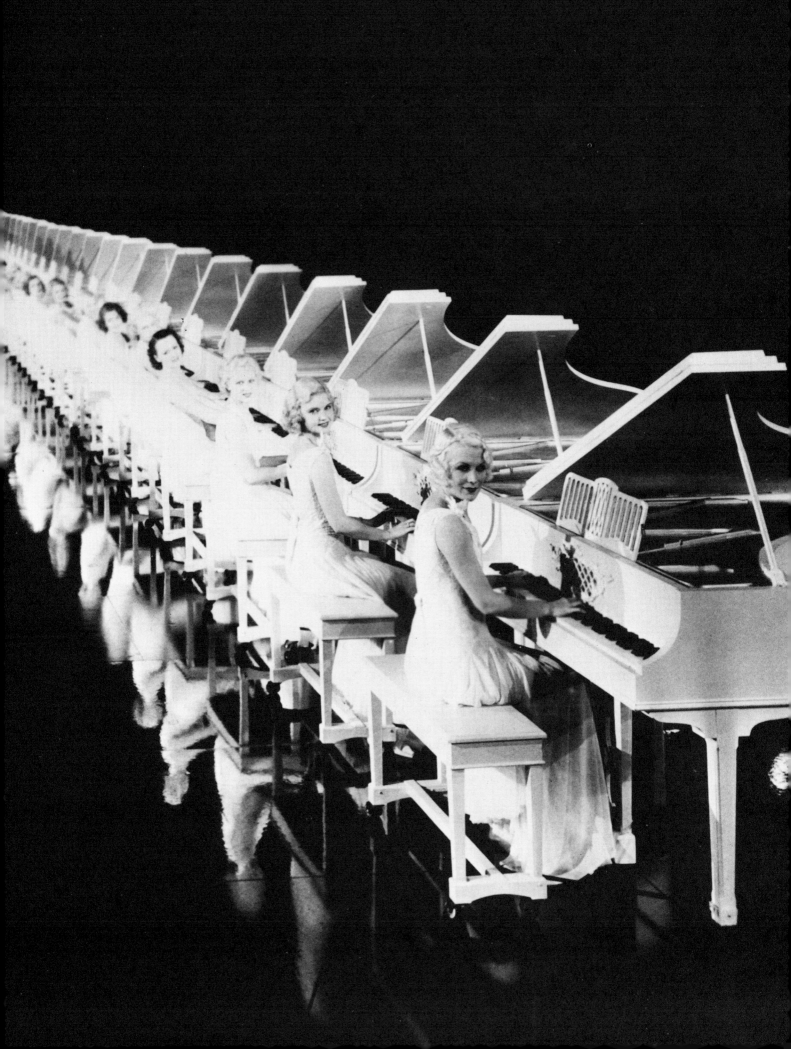

Louise and Joan take a trip to Italy, and in Venice they hear a gondolier with a splendid voice, who happens to be Powell. He has gone along with a scheme to be discovered and imported. Dick is soon back in New York as the singing star of a program sponsored by Flagenheim's Odorless Cheese, and he rises to fame. But soon he can't stand the deception any more and has to admit who he is. However, by that time it doesn't matter.

The seven Warren-Dubin songs include a humorous commercial for the cheese and a cheeky song with a jazzy beat that was to become a standard—"Lulu's Back in Town":

Got-ta get my old tux - e-do pressed,_ got-ta sew a but-ton on my vest,_'Cause to-night I've got - ta look my best,_ Lu-lu's back in town._____

Broadway Gondolier derived most of its fun from digging at commercial radio. And as in *Twenty Million Sweethearts*, Powell was again supported by the Mills Brothers and the orchestra of Ted Fiorita. The song that made the best impression was "The Rose in Her Hair," which clearly reveals Harry Warren's Italian heritage. Sung partly in Italian by Powell, the song sounds very much as if it might have been born on the canals of Venice:

In her eyes there was moon-light,_____ and a rose in her hair,_____

"The Rose in Her Hair" didn't make much impression on Hal Wallis, the head of production at Warners—to him it sounded "short." This didn't worry Harry Warren much. "By now I'd learned that Wallis and Jack Warner differed in their points of view," he says. "If Wallis didn't like a song I'd go to Jack and say, 'I just played this for Hal, and he thinks we should drop it from the picture.' After he'd heard it he'd say, 'What the hell does he know? Leave it in.' I'd do exactly the same thing in reverse if Jack didn't like a song and get the same reaction from Wallis. That way I got to use everything we wrote."

PAGE MISS GLORY (1935)

After a dozen years of basing his Cosmopolitan Pictures at MGM, William Randolph Hearst made a deal with Warner Bros. and moved his operation to their lot. The deal included his primary movie asset, star-mistress Marion Davies. The move would prove to be a mistake, and after only four pictures at Warners her career was over.

The first of these movies was *Page Miss Glory*, which starred her with Dick Powell and gave him just one song to sing. The feeble story concerns a promoter, Pat O'Brien, who sends a composite photograph to a beauty contest, calling his entry Dawn Glory, and wins. In his haste to come up with someone who resembles the photograph, he seizes upon hotel chambermaid Davies and manages to transform her into a national beauty. An aviation hero falls in love with the photo, and when Davies sees him she falls too. Despite such thin material, Warren and Dubin were sufficiently inspired to come up with a cheery song:

When the moon is new____ I al-ways make a lit-tle wish or two____ ____ And when I want some-one to tell them to, what do I do? I page Miss Glo-ry.

Harry Warren recalls the Marion Davies arrival on the Warner lot: "They brought her bungalow from MGM, all the way from Culver City to Burbank, about a dozen miles, and it took a couple of days. It was a huge thing, and I remember passing it on Sunset Boulevard on the way home. It was moving at snail's pace with men walking in front and alongside with lanterns. And then they planted it right alongside the music department. This turned out to be all right, because she was very hospitable, and we all spent a lot of time on lunches that went on for hours.

"She had her own group of musicians with her, and they used to play her on to the set with stately marches and then some romantic music to put her in the mood to act. People were afraid of her at first, but she proved to be down to earth, humorous, and very kind to the working people.

"Hearst was there all the time. He didn't contribute much in the way of advice or direction—he just sat and watched Marion. And it was amusing to see Dick Powell trying to make love to her for the scenes, with Hearst looking on. I think poor Dick must have been shaking in his boots."

In a Witmark office in New York, Eddie Duchin gives a private performance of several Warren and Dubin songs to an interested couple.

The Gold Diggers of 1935: Harry Warren with Busby Berkeley and Wini Shaw at their first rehearsal of "The Lullaby of Broadway."

SHIPMATES FOREVER (1935)

Ship - mates, stand to - geth - er, Don't give up the ship;

Dick Powell and Ruby Keeler had done so well by *Flirtation Walk*, set in the U.S. Military Academy at West Point, that a sequel set in the Naval Academy at Annapolis was almost inevitable. Dubin and Warren were pressed into service, and their stirring marching song for the midshipmen was quickly adopted by the academy as their service song.

The picture has a good atmosphere, and although it might have been very corny, it was kept in line by a superior director, Frank Borzage, who had also directed *Flirtation Walk*. This time Powell is the son of an admiral, Lewis Stone, who expects his boy to follow the family tradition and become a naval officer. Powell doesn't care for this course and prefers to make his living as a singer. But he finally gives in, because of the love and persuasion of Ruby, who teaches dancing to the children of the academy's officers.

The other cadets at first resent him, but when he heroically saves the life of one of them in a boiler-room mishap, they change their minds, and Dick realizes that his duty is with the navy.

Shipmates Forever is more a romance than a musical. This was a relief to Warren and Dubin, who barely had any time off in 1935. In an early sequence in a New York nightclub where he is employed, Powell directs a song at Ruby:

Ev - 'ry-time your lips say "No, Sir!" I won't lis - ten, I'm too wise,

I would rath - er lis - ten to your eyes._____

Later he and Ruby pledge their loyalty to each other with a song that avoids the usual slow and tender style and instead takes up a naval drill theme with a jaunty beat:

If you're the Cap - tain, I'll be the crew,

'Cause I'd just love to take or - ders from you;_____

The fans liked *Shipmates Forever*, and it seemed to Warren, Dubin, Powell, and Keeler that the wave of movie musicals would never end. This was one of just six pictures in which Powell appeared in 1935. Says Warren, "My wife was always complaining that I was never home. I couldn't get home much of the time. Working for Warners was like being in the service."

STARS OVER BROADWAY (1935)

Stars over Broadway is of interest mainly to admirers of the virile American tenor James Melton (1904–61). He made his screen debut in this film, following a good reputation in opera and a considerable following as a middlebrow singer on radio. Much of the ninety minutes of this picture is occupied by music, with five songs by Warren and Dubin, Schubert's "Ave Maria," arias from *Aïda* and *Martha*, and the Western ballad "Carry Me Back to the Lone Prairie," which Melton kept in his repertoire.

The Gold Diggers of 1935: Wini Shaw, Dick Powell and umpteen dancers doing "The Lullaby of Broadway."

The Gold Diggers of 1935: Dick Powell sings "I'm Going Shopping With You," but rich Gloria Stuart picks up the tabs.

Busby Berkeley was assigned to help director William Keighley stage the musical sequences, but aside from "At Your Service, Madame," staged in a nightclub with a floor the size of an airplane hangar, there isn't much of the Berkeley touch.

This is the film for which Warren wrote "September in the Rain." Berkeley intended to choreograph this song with a forest of movable silver trees, but the studio decided not to go ahead with it, probably feeling that the cost would not be in line with the returns on the film. Berkeley's staging of "Broadway Cinderella" was completely filmed but cut from the final print, much to the chagrin of Warren, who had come up with another of his flowing Italianate love songs:

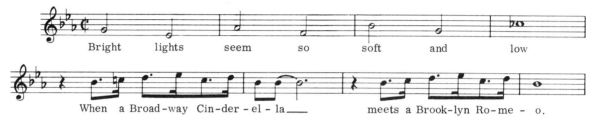

The plot of *Stars over Broadway* concerns Pat O'Brien, once more the slick promoter, turning a hotel porter (Melton) into a radio star but keeping him from his true interest—opera. Despite his success, Melton takes to drinking, with O'Brien eventually realizing the error of his ways and sending the young tenor off to Italy for the necessary operatic training. The film also marked the movie debut of Jane Froman, but her career in pictures was fleeting because she had great difficulty speaking lines.

None of the new songs became hits, but one of them, "Where Am I?" has remained a favorite among musicians, who feel its melodic line lends itself to intrumental playing, particularly for woodwinds:

COLLEEN (1936)

Colleen was the last of the Powell-Keeler musicals and the least interesting. None of its four Warren-Dubin songs became popular. Says Harry Warren, "Ruby Keeler was, and is, a very nice woman, but she was a reluctant movie star. She was very honest about her talent, that she really couldn't act or sing and she couldn't understand why she had been so popular. She never discussed Jolson, but we all thought life with him must have been a strain for her, and I think by the time she did this picture she was getting tired of the business."

Ms. Keeler made only one more picture for Warners, *Ready, Willing and Able*, and after a couple of minor films for Columbia she retired. More than thirty years would elapse before she could be enticed to make a comeback, in the greatly successful revival of *No, No, Nanette*.

On the set of *The Gold Diggers of 1935:* conductor
Ray Heindorf, pianist Martin Fried, Busby Berkeley,
Leo Forbstein, Harry Warren and Dick Powell.

The highlight of *Colleen* is the sprightly song "You Gotta Know How to Dance," with
Keeler dancing with Paul Draper and trying unsuccessfully to persuade Powell that he should
be a dancer too:

The plot of *Colleen* has Hugh Herbert, a mainstay of so many Warner musicals, as an
eccentric millionaire who scandalizes his family by adopting gold digger Joan Blondell and
putting her in charge of his dress shop. His more practical nephew, Powell, hires Ruby and
puts her in charge. Eventually the family buys Herbert out, and they all sail for Europe on a
liner, which turns out to have Ruby on board, followed by the inevitable Keeler-Powell
romance. Jack Oakie figures in all this limp nonsense as a brash promoter–press agent and
sings a cheeky song, "A Boulevardier from the Bronx."

Powell sings two love songs. One of them, "An Evening with You," has a slightly naughty
ring to it:

In the other, which is more romantic, Powell smoothly croons his satisfaction at having
found the love of his life:

79

Go Into Your Dance: Helen Morgan singing "The Little Things You Used to Do," accompanied by Martin Fried.

Go Into Your Dance: Al Jolson performing "A Quarter to Nine," as Ruby Keeler makes her entrance from behind.

HEARTS DIVIDED (1936)

Two lone - ly hearts di - vid - ed, but some day those hearts— shall beat—— as one,

Warners gave Dick Powell's vocal cords very little rest. He and Marion Davies had become good friends, and would remain so until her death in 1961, and she asked for him for her next picture. This proved unfortunate, because the part was beyond Powell's range at that time and he appeared slightly ridiculous with a coiffure and wearing nineteenth-century pantaloons.

The screenplay was based on Rida Johnson Young's play *Glorious Betsy*, which dealt with the adventures of Baltimore belle Betsy Patterson. In the film version Powell plays Captain Jerome Bonaparte, the younger brother of Napoleon. While on a diplomatic mission to the United States he falls in love with Betsy and declines the royal marriage his brother has arranged for him.

He takes Betsy to Paris, but while there Napoleon asks for a private meeting with her and persuades her to give up Jerome. She regretfully complies, but the ardent Jerome follows her back to Baltimore and plights his troth.

The film did little to arrest the decline of Marion Davies' career. Its best moments are those using two love ballads, "Two Hearts Divided" and "My Kingdom for a Kiss," both written in a deliberately old-fashioned romantic style.

Warren recalls that "My Kingdom for a Kiss" met with the approval of the esteemed Erich Wolfgang Korngold, who had shifted from writing operas in Vienna to writing film scores at Warners. "He was a stout, humorous, and totally Viennese character, a really marvelous guy. After he had seen this picture he would start humming my melody every time we passed each other on the lot. He would hum the first few measures, nod his head at me, and say, 'Good.' I got a big kick out of that."

My king - dom for a kiss,——— I'd glad - ly give you,———

—— My king - dom just for this,——— A kiss from you,

CAIN AND MABEL (1936)

The critics pointed out that Marion Davies' acting in *Hearts Divided* was somewhat undermined because she was obviously a woman with a lusty sense of humor which she had trouble keeping submerged in playing a young patrician. She was by this time thirty-eight. She and William Randolph Hearst, who doted on her and was blind to any shortcomings, decided to make her next picture a little more earthy. To help with box-office appeal they brought Clark Gable over from MGM.

Unfortunately, *Cain and Mabel* didn't do much for either Davies or Gable. In this one she plays a waitress named Mabel O'Dare, who is picked up and promoted into the musical theater by a brash newspaperman (Roscoe Karns this time) and comes to the attention of a boxer,

Go Into Your Dance: The song is "Mammy, I'll Sing About You." Guess who sang it?

In Caliente: Phil Regan serenades
Dolores Del Rio with "Muchacha."

83

Broadway Gondolier: Taxi driver Dick Powell, impressario Adolphe Menjou and radio station receptionist Joan Blondell.

Broadway Gondolier: Dick Powell as the fake Venetian tenor. The bandleader is Ted Fiorito.

Broadway Gondolier: Radio idol Dick Powell surrounded by adoring fans. To the right of him: Adolphe Menjou, Louise Fazenda and Grant Mitchell.

Page Miss Glory: Dick Powell and Marion Davies.

Shipmates Forever: Ruby Keeler and Dick Powell.

Shipmates Forever: Dick Powell and Ruby Keeler, singing and dancing to "I'd Love to Take Orders From You."

Larry Cain, when her tap dancing in the hotel room above his keeps him awake. Cain and Mabel are both unwilling stars in their trades, trying to make enough money to get out. The newspaperman promotes a romance between them, for publicity purposes, but eventually they actually do fall in love and find the happy retreat they crave.

Marion Davies was better suited to playing a showgirl than a society belle, but her dancing and singing were barely good enough to get her through the picture. In an early sequence she rehearses and performs the production number "Coney Island," which is set in a fun fair and involves Davies performing with various characters, including figures in a wax museum who come to life. Bobby Connolly's direction of this sequence is rather heavy-handed, and it goes on for six and a half minutes.

I can't for-get the night I met you down at Con - ey Is - land.

The principal production number in *Cain and Mabel* is "I'll Sing You a Thousand Love Songs," which gained lasting popularity, although Warren and Dubin considered it one of their more ordinary creations. "Neither Al nor I were very happy with it," Warren says, "and we decided the best thing to do would be to pump it up with some other love songs. Hearst made it known that he wanted this to be a truly great production number and that no expense was to be spared. It was his money.

"They built a huge set to accommodate a Venetian canal, with bridges and movable sections of scenery, and a huge organ. All this required raising the whole floor of the sound stage by about five feet. It must have cost them a fortune. They had a swarm of extras all in costume and a big mixed choir, with Marion not much more than a model in this thing. A real gilding of the lily. Since they wanted it to be long—the edited version runs eight minutes—Dubin and I had the arrangers interpolate 'L'Amour, Toujours L'Amour,' 'Those Endearing Young

Shipmates Forever: Admiral Lewis Stone looks on approvingly as Dick and Ruby say it with a kiss at Annapolis—just before everybody breaks into a final chorus of "Don't Give Up the Ship."

Stars Over Broadway: James Melton

Stars Over Broadway: Marie Wilson
and Frank McHugh.

87

Charms,' and a couple of our own tunes, 'The Shadow Waltz' and 'The Rose in Her Hair,' which sounded good sung in Italian by a gondolier. We had become weary of these elongated versions of our songs in the Berkeley productions, so we thought we would give this melody a little relief."

I'll sing you a thou - sand love songs And still they'll seem so few, For I need a' thou - sand voic - es, To tell you how I love you,

Marion Davies made just one more picture, *Ever Since Eve*, and then it was all over. Now forty, rich, and wise enough to realize that she had nothing more to contribute to the movies, she retired to her chief role, as the mistress of San Simeon. Says Warren, "I never worked for or with a nicer woman. She was never a problem, and she was so kind and generous to everybody, even the extras, that we were sorry to see her go."

GOLD DIGGERS OF 1937 (1936)

Being called in to write songs for pictures to which other songwriters had been assigned proved a growing embarrassment for Warren and Dubin, particularly in the case of *Gold Diggers of 1937*. Harold Arlen and E. Y. Harburg had signed a one-year contract with Warners and had previously scored Jolson's *The Singing Kid* and the Powell-Blondell *Stage Struck*. Lloyd Bacon was given the new *Gold Diggers* to direct, with Busby Berkeley inevitably assigned to devise the production numbers. Of the four Arlen-Harburg songs, Berkeley claimed none gave him a basis for anything fanciful, and he asked Jack Warner to put Warren and Dubin on the picture.

"This was very uncomfortable," says Warren. "Arlen and Harburg were top-notch talents, really gifted men, and we had all been friends for years. It was good to be appreciated by Berkeley, but it was tough trying to convince Harold and Yip that the whole thing hadn't been our idea. I don't think Buzz either knew or cared much about music. I guess he was a little superstitious, and maybe he felt confident with us. Whatever it was, he wouldn't do the picture until we agreed to write something for him."

Arlen and Harburg left Warners after writing their songs, two of which were dropped, and as Edward Jablonski writes in his book on Arlen, *Happy with the Blues*, "The year had given them valuable insights into the ways and means of working in Hollywood."

The plot of *Gold Diggers of 1937* is a shade better than the others, possibly because it was based on the Broadway play *Sweet Mystery of Life*, which was about backstage machinations in the theater. Dick Powell is an insurance agent inveigled by chiselers into selling a one-million-dollar policy to a hypochondriac theatrical producer, dodderingly and deftly played by Victor Moore. Powell really doesn't like the insurance game and is a show-biz type at heart, and when he realizes what he has done he does his best to keep Moore in good health and even takes over the production of his show. He is aided in this by showgirl-turned-secretary Joan Blondell, whom he persuades to return to her real bent.

Colleen: Ruby Keeler and Paul Draper.

Colleen: Dick Powell and Ruby Keeler.

89

Stars Over Broadway: Harry Warren and James Melton on the set.

Colleen: That's Dick Powell blowing the trumpet in the center, with Paul Draper at left and Ruby Keeler at the right.

Colleen: Most of "An Evening With You" was sung outdoors by Dick Powell, with the Warner orchestra providing immediate accompaniment. Ray Heindorf conducts and Harry Warren just leans against the piano.

Hearts Divided: Dick Powell and Marion Davies.

On the set of *Hearts Divided* Dick Powell checks a song with Harry Warren, who can't remember why he had his hand on the typewriter.

The picture opens with a spirited song for the Gold Diggers, "With Plenty of Money and You," reflecting the growing optimism of the post-Depression United States:

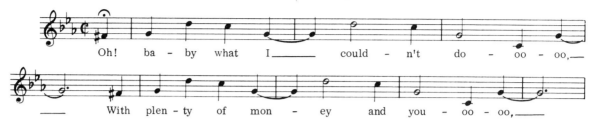

Oh! ba - by what I____ could - n't do - oo - oo,____
____ With plen - ty of mon - ey and you - oo - oo,____

Warners was forever nagging Busby Berkeley about production costs, and for his big number in this picture he struck upon an effective and relatively inexpensive way of staging a spectacular routine. He used a large group of girls in military marching formations. The idea came, as almost always, from Al Dubin, who thought of a song using the war between men and women as its theme. According to Warren, Dubin was not happily married, and the cryptic comments in the lyrics tend to support that opinion:

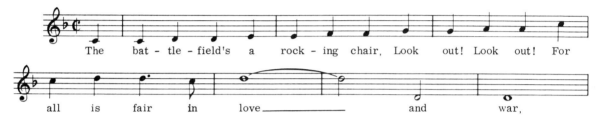

The bat - tle - field's a rock - ing chair, Look out! Look out! For
all is fair in love____ and war,

Later in the song Dubin advises us:

> And with your back against the wall,
> She marches you to City Hall,
> And leads you through the door.
> And then the deed is done,
> Her victory is won,
> For love is just like war.

Berkeley was on home ground with a song like this. He had already been married several times, and his skill with military formations was something he had first developed in the army in France, to while away the hours of boredom in camps.

As for Warren, he says, "I love marches. I grew up with the sounds of bands, with drums and brass ringing in my ears. I'll write a march for anyone at the drop of a downbeat." Warren thinks that it was while doing *Gold Diggers of 1937* that he and Dubin turned out two songs for the Joe E. Brown comedy, *Sons o' Guns*. One was "For a Buck and a Quarter a Day," sung by Brown, and the other was for Wini Shaw, "In the Arms of an Army Man," but nothing came of either song.

SING ME A LOVE SONG (1936)

James Melton's second film was no more impressive than the first, with even lower production values. However, as a pleasant little program picture and part of a double bill on Warners' guaranteed block-booking system, it doubtless returned its investment. In this one Melton is a playboy who inherits a department store and then, under an assumed name, takes a job in it as a clerk to find out what it's all about. In the process he finds the love of a solid working girl, Patricia Ellis—with Hugh Herbert thrown in for laughs as a kleptomaniac.

92

Cain and Mabel: Part of the set for the staging of "I'll Sing You a Thousand Love Songs," with Marion Davies being given the gondola treatment.

Cain and Mabel: William Randolph Hearst spared no expense in giving his Marion, (center foreground) a lavish musical. But it did little to halt her rapidly deflating career.

Warren and Dubin supplied three songs, with four others drawn from the standard repertoire, making this picture as much a songfest as a light comedy. The most lighthearted piece in the picture is a comic patter, "That's the Least You Can Do for the Lady," but far more typical of Melton's style is the ballad "The Little House That Love Built," clearly tailored to suit Melton's lyric tenor:

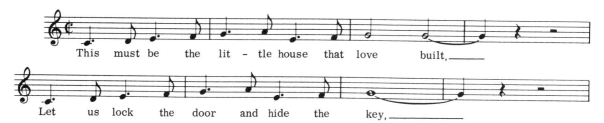

This must be the lit - tle house that love built,____

Let us lock the door and hide the key,____

Sing Me a Love Song is also the home of one of Warren's most respected melodies. "Summer Night" has never become part of the standard selection of songs, but it is nonetheless a particular favorite of other songwriters and musicians. Seemingly simple in melodic line, the song is a flow of natural cadences and could only be the work of someone with an innate sense of music.

Sum - mer night,____ star - ry skies,____ You can see my sweet-heart

with a thou - sand eyes,____ Why have I____ on - ly

two____ To be - hold a thou-sand charms I i - dol - ize?

MELODY FOR TWO (1937)

There's a sound of a wa-ter-fall____ In my mel-o-dy for two,____

Warners quickly put James Melton in another picture, perhaps to try to boost his appeal with moviegoers or perhaps to try to use up his three-picture contract as quickly as possible. The attempt to make a movie star of him failed, and after this film he never again took an acting role on the screen. Says Warren, "It was a pity, because Melton was both a very nice man and a marvelous singer. That was my kind of singer, and it was a pleasure to write for him—you knew that he could sing anything you gave him and that it would be done with skill and taste. I wish I could say that of all the people I worked with."

However, Melton never lacked for work in radio, recitals, and opera houses. In *Melody for Two*, which has a beautifully lyric title song, he appeared as a band leader with a rather narrow mind who argues with his arranger and objects to playing the arrangements. It was hardly a guise in which Melton could endear himself to moviegoers. Once again Patricia Ellis was his leading lady, playing a singer who straightens him out.

Three other songs were added to the two supplied by Warren and Dubin, but of the five only one stood out—and stood out so clearly that it gradually became recognized as a classic American song. This was "September in the Rain." The melody had been written two years before for *Stars over Broadway*, in which it can be heard in the background.

Explains Warren, "It came about because Leo Forbstein was always asking me for tunes he could sprinkle here and there in pictures, in addition to the songs. He had a favorite expression, 'Give me thirty-two bars of schmaltz.' Leo liked to have lots of music in pictures, and he always asked me to write tunes for love scenes. I seldom put titles on these pieces, and a lot of the time I never knew what happened to them. If I'd been more businesslike I should have, but I didn't, and I could never refuse Leo. But by this time I was like a dog chasing his tail, with so many songs going in so many pictures.

"It was Dubin who came up with the title "September in the Rain," which I liked, and I wrote the melody from the title. We saved it until we thought we had the right spot, and with Jimmie Melton the song couldn't have got off to a better start."

The Warren-Dubin duties called more and more for supplying single songs for use in dramatic pictures, such as *Marked Woman*, with Bette Davis, and *Stolen Holiday*, with Kay Francis, but the songs were always lost items.

The Gold Diggers of 1937: Dick Powell and Joan Blondell.

The Gold Diggers of 1937: Joan Blondell heads up the parade in Berkeley's treatment of "All's Fair in Love and War."

THE SINGING MARINE (1937)

Since Dick Powell had been in the army in *Flirtation Walk* and in the navy in *Shipmates Forever*, it was certain that sooner or later he would turn up in the uniform of a marine. Unfortunately, Ruby Keeler couldn't or wouldn't appear in *The Singing Marine,* and Warners substituted the pretty but lackluster Doris Weston.

Somehow the picture didn't quite work up the spirit of the former pictures. Ray Enright directed, and Busby Berkeley was brought in to add his unique touch, which is apparent only in the "Night over Shanghai" sequence. Warren and Dubin wrote one of their bigger scores, a full six songs, but even there the results were disappointing. The song intended as the hit ballad, "I Know Now," was given to the leading lady instead of to Powell, and it fell flat in her throat. The overcute "The Lady Who Wouldn't Be Kissed" was handed to Lee Dixon to sing and dance, but Dixon lacked charisma.

The burden of the film fell on Powell, and he could have used some help.

Here Powell is a bashful Arkansas-born marine, whose buddies appreciate his singing because it helps put their girlfriends in an amorous mood when they go for wienie roasts on the beach. Strumming a guitar, Dick softly croons:

You can't run a - way from love to - night, Not while there's a moon a-bove to - night,

His barracks chums enter the singing marine in a radio contest, and they send him off to New York with his girlfriend, who is also a singer. She doesn't make the grade, but Dick clicks with a snappy love song:

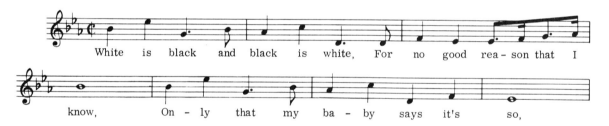

White is black and black is white, For no good rea - son that I know, On - ly that my ba - by says it's so,

Sing Me a Love Song: Patricia Ellis and James Melton.

Sing Me a Love Song: Allen Jenkins, Zasu Pitts, James Melton and Patricia Ellis.

Melody for Two: Patricia Ellis checks a song with Warren and Dubin.

Melody for Two: Patricia Ellis.

Harry Warren discusses a song with
James Melton on the set of *Melody
for Two.*

102

This leads to a radio contract and tremendous popularity, which turns Dick from bashful-confused to edgy-temperamental. Called back into the service, he is shipped to the Far East, where his friends go sour on him for trying to continue his radio career and quit the corps.

At one point he wanders into a nightclub in Shanghai, which gave Berkeley cause to launch into another of his fantasies. "Night over Shanghai," with a lyric by Johnny Mercer—Warren's first Warners song away from Dubin—is an excellent piece of material, a superior, almost operatic song full of minor modes and a sultry, quite Oriental feeling:

Night____ ov - er Shang - hai,____ Moon____ on the rise,____

"Night over Shanghai" lacks the sparkle of "Shanghai Lil," but it has its own sense of drama and color, with a valuable contribution from harmonica player Larry Adler. The Mercer lyrics speak of "pale yellow faces with sad old eyes" and of "dreams gone up in smoke . . . where are the dreamers who never awoke?"

To no one's surprise Dick decides to stick with the corps and give up the idea of being an entertainer. He joins his comrades in a rousing rendition of "The Song of the Marines," a song the marine corps later adopted:

O - ver the sea let's go, men!_____ We're shov - in' right off, we're shov - in' right off a - gain,

Johnny Mercer wrote the lyrics for "Night over Shanghai" because of Al Dubin's prolonged absence. "Al was getting more and more tired of working for Warners," Warren says. "He was always disappearing, and we would never know where he was. He did his writing away from the lot, and after these absences he would return with the lyrics. But he didn't make the deadline for "Shanghai," and Johnny Mercer happened to be on the spot.

"Some months before this Hal Wallis had asked me if I knew of a good team of songwriters and I'd suggested Richard Whiting and Johnny. I'd known Dick for years—he'd written 'Till We Meet Again' and 'The Japanese Sandman' back during the World War, and he'd done a lot of songs for pictures—but he needed a lyricist, and Johnny seemed right. He was young and eager, and he'd had a hit with his 'I'm an Old Cowhand.' So Warners signed them, which took some of the pressure off of us."

Whiting and Mercer proved to be a felicitous teaming, and in a year or so they wrote a flock for songs for *Ready, Willing and Able, Hollywood Hotel,* and *Varsity Show.* Suddenly and tragically death ended the partnership, when Whiting died in February 1938 at forty-seven.

SAN QUENTIN (1937)

A movie about penal reform was hardly a likely birthplace for a love song, but Warner production chief Hal Wallis required one for heroine Ann Sheridan. She had been under contract to the studio for more than a year doing bit parts, and Warners now took a chance on giving her a lead. In *San Quentin* she appears as a nightclub singer and the sister of criminal Humphrey Bogart, who is sent to prison. Pat O'Brien is the yard captain at the prison, and he and Sheridan fall in love.

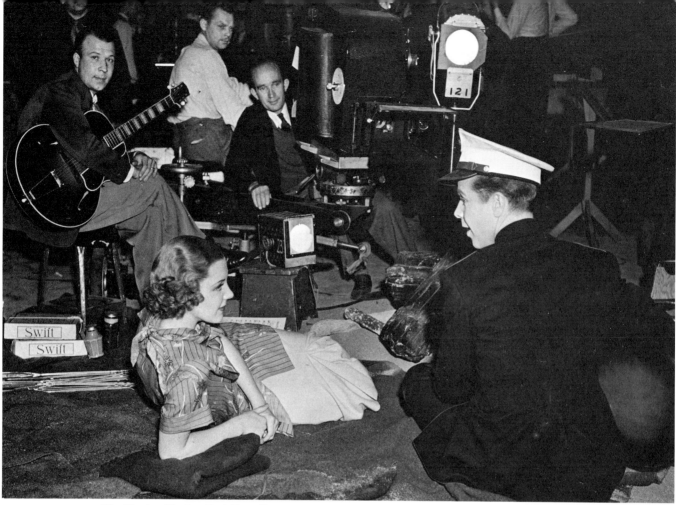

The Singing Marine: Dick Powell croons "You Can't Run Away from Love Tonight" to Doris Weston on what is supposed to be a beach. The gent with the glasses in the top left corner is Harry Warren, who liked to hang around to see what they were doing with his songs.

Agent Hugh Herbert gives *The Singing Marine* his card right after hearing him sing " 'Cause My Baby Says It's So." Doris Weston didn't draw any offers with her singing, but she did win the marine.

The Singing Marine: Lee Dixon, singing and dancing about "The Lady Who Wouldn't be Kissed."

The Singing Marine and his buddies belting our "The Song of the Marines."

Recalls Harry Warren, "Wallis came into our office and told us they had decided to give Ann the star treatment. He said, 'I want you to write a hit song for her.' Wallis is one of the greatest producers Hollywood has ever had, but I don't think he had the faintest idea what went into writing songs. Ordering a hit didn't seem out of line to him. I asked him if he knew the picture was going to be a hit, and he just gave me that funny smile of his. So we wrote 'How Could You?' for Ann. It did fairly well, but it was no smash hit. If I'd known the secret to sitting down and writing hits, I'd have been the richest man in the history of music."

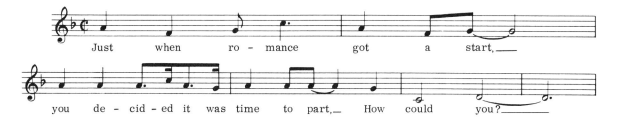

Just when ro - mance got a start,____

you de - cid - ed it was time to part,__ How could you?_____

MR. DODD TAKES THE AIR (1937)

In giving Kenny Baker the lead in *Mr. Dodd Takes the Air*, Warners again tried to make a movie star out of a popular radio singer—with the same disappointing results they had had with James Melton. However, Harry Warren looks back on the picture with some satisfaction. "Kenny was a very pleasant fellow," Warren says, "and like Melton he had had excellent musical training, which made writing for him a pleasure. He told me he'd got his start a couple of years before when he won a singing contest by singing our 'The Rose in Her Hair.' He was lucky for us on this picture, because we wrote 'Remember Me?' for him, and it brought us an Oscar nomination. I liked working on this picture, and we did one song I was really crazy about, 'The Girl You Used to Be,' but it never caught on."

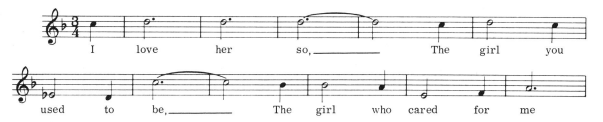

I love her so,_____ The girl you

used to be,_____ The girl who cared for me

The fact that Harry Warren is "crazy about" sentimental ballads like "The Girl You Used to Be" is, in the opinion of his friends, a clear indication of the nature of the man, which is very gentle and sentimental.

In *Mr. Dodd Takes the Air*, Kenny Baker is first seen as a small-town electrician who sings for his friends and is overheard by some radio executives. They take him to New York, where he suffers an attack of bronchitis. A quack doctor tampers with his tonsils and turns him from a baritone into a tenor. The sponsors fire him, thinking that the public will be disappointed, but the opposite happens, and they have to hire him back.

As in all the Warner pictures with a radio setting, the sound medium receives a good deal of ribbing. Through it all the innocent Baker is loved and saved from exploitation by an office girl—Jane Wyman in her first leading role after many Warner bits.

Baker sings one operatic aria by Donizetti, plus the four Warren-Dubin songs, one of which is a lullaby, "Here Comes the Sandman." "Remember Me" quickly became, and stayed, a hit.

106

San Quentin: Ann Sheridan singing "How Could You?"

Harry Warren checks the sheet music of "September in the Rain" with Al Dubin. The piece to the right is the one they wrote for Ann Sheridan to sing in *San Quentin,* "How Could You?"

107

Mr. Dodd Takes the Air: Radio station receptionist Jane Wyman, agent Frank McHugh and hopeful singer Kenny Baker.

Mr. Dodd Takes the Air: Kenny Baker and Guy Kibbee.

Mr. Dodd Takes the Air: Here Mr. Dodd takes a bow as Jane Wyman beams her approval.

The Baker voice also moved the songwriters to come up with yet another sentimental ballad, a pretty one but not destined for permanence:

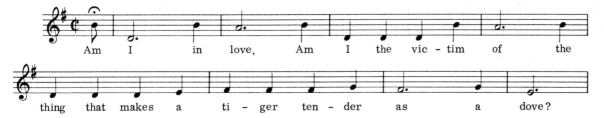

Am I in love, Am I the vic - tim of the thing that makes a ti - ger ten - der as a dove?

COWBOY FROM BROOKLYN (1938)

Dick Powell had been complaining more and more about being put into nothing but musicals. He had yet to appear in a movie in which he didn't sing. In 1937 he had placed in the first ten in box-office popularity, and he felt that that gave him the right to better material. Warners, on the other hand, believed that a star should stick with the kind of material that had made him a star.

A partial concession was to let Powell do a little more light comedy, of which *Cowboy from Brooklyn* is a meager example. Here Powell is a drifter who gets a job on a dude ranch and while singing for the guests is heard by a slick promoter—Pat O'Brien again!—and turned into a singing cowboy on radio. A small amount of comedy arises from his phobia of all animals.

Richard Whiting and Johnny Mercer were assigned as the songwriters, but Whiting was stricken with illness before the score was completed and died. One more song—the title song—was needed, and Harry Warren stepped in to join Mercer:

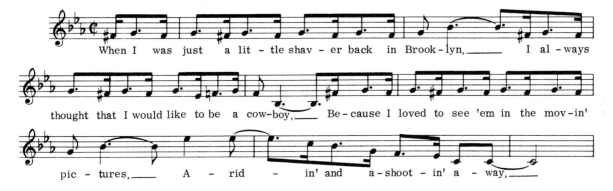

When I was just a lit - tle shav - er back in Brook - lyn,_____ I al - ways thought that I would like to be a cow-boy,____ Be - cause I loved to see 'em in the mov - in' pic - tures,____ A - rid - in' and a-shoot - in' a - way,_____

THE GOLD DIGGERS IN PARIS (1938)

By early 1938 it was apparent that the big, splashy Warner musicals were on the wane. The need for fantasies to lift the spirits of the Depression was no more, and Dick Powell refused to appear in *The Gold Diggers in Paris*.

Warners still had a commitment with Rudy Vallee, and here was the obvious place to spend it. Busby Berkeley was called in to do a few production numbers but cautioned to not make them expensive. With Johnny Mercer at loose ends because of Whiting's death, Warners signed him to the picture along with Al Dubin, which added to Dubin's growing unrest.

Harry Warren gives Kenny Baker his own version of "Remember Me?" during the making of *Mr. Dodd Takes the Air.*

Cowboy from Brooklyn: Priscilla Lane and Dick Powell.

Of the two Warren-Mercer songs only "Day Dreaming" brought them any royalties, mostly because Vallee recorded it and performed it on his radio program. The song was clearly cut to fit Vallee's light, crooning style:

All night long I'm day - dream - ing, day - dream - ing of won-der-ful you,—

The plot of *The Gold Diggers in Paris* leans heavily on the tired device of mistaken identity, with Vallee and his band of entertainers being invited by the French government to appear at the Paris Exposition, assuming them to be connected with the American Ballet Company.

The Vallee group manage to make a good impression, thanks to several spirited Warren-Dubin numbers, with Berkeley displaying his visual tricks in "The Latin Quarter." Once Vallee gets through with the lyrics, squads of dancers prance around the Warner concept of the Left Bank.

So this is gay Pa - ree!— Come on a - long with me,—

— We're step - ping out to see— the Lat - in Quar - ter,

Rudy Vallee and his troupe arrive in a very Warner Bros.-backlot version of Paris for *The Gold Diggers in Paris.*

In "A Stranger in Paris" Vallee croons about the glories of the City of Light, but a far more entertaining song is "I Wanna Go Back to Bali," in which Dubin gets in some witty barbs about the dubious pleasures of the South Pacific paradise.

I wan-na go back to Ba-li, ___ To the is-land of sun-ny skies, ___ You can see those scenes in mag-a-zines, but you nev-er can see the flies,

The Gold Diggers in Paris did fairly good business, but the handwriting was beginning to appear faintly on the wall that an era was drawing to a close.

GARDEN OF THE MOON (1938)

Busby Berkeley was entirely responsible for directing *Garden of the Moon*, although he is not much remembered for this film, since it has little of his lavish touch. It was also his last musical for Warners and one of the very few turned out by the studio in the 1938–39 period. Johnny Mercer was still under contract, and with nothing for him to do Warners assigned him to this picture in addition to Al Dubin, forcing the two lyricists to collaborate.

The title refers to a nightclub, operated by shrewd, tough Pat O'Brien, who hires a young bandleader, John Payne, and constantly quarrels with him about material and methods. But they do agree on one point, that the club has a good theme song:

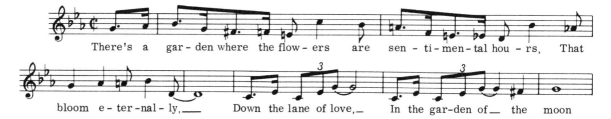

There's a gar-den where the flow-ers are sen-ti-men-tal hou-rs, That bloom e-ter-nal-ly, ___ Down the lane of love, ___ In the gar-den of ___ the moon

Curt Bois leads his ballet company for their performance in *The Gold Diggers in Paris*.

Most of the action in *Garden of the Moon* takes place in the club and is built around the banter between O'Brien and Payne, with the love interest supplied by Margaret Lindsay, as a press agent who invents publicity stories for Payne and falls in love with him, to the chagrin of O'Brien.

None of the five Warren melodies became standards, but several are of the kind collected by song enthusiasts. The nearest to a hit was "Love is Where You Find It," which is unfortunately confused with another song of that title:

Oh! Love_____ is where you find it, No mat - ter where you go,_____ You may_____ be in Ka - lu - a, or Ko - ko - mo,__

The most memorable song from *Garden of the Moon*—again an item for film buffs rather than the general public—is "The Girl Friend of the Whirling Dervish," a wild, campy bit about a saucy girl who gives her master the "runaround . . . while he's out making an honest rupee, she's out making whoopee." Payne sings the main lyric and conducts the band, which is actually that of Joe Venuti, and Johnny "Scat" Davis and Jerry Colonna chime in with some of the more bizarre bits of business:

She's the girl friend_ of the whirl-ing der - vish,__ She's the sweet-est one he's found,

Says Warren, "I thought this was one of the more amusing of the pictures we did at Warners, but it was a sad experience for Dubin. He had been forced to write with Mercer, and he felt insulted, and Johnny understood this. He couldn't do anything about it. It was just another example of the insensitivity of the movie producers in dealing with talent. I always had the feeling they looked upon songwriters as a lower species.

"Dubin had been unhappy for a long time at Warners, and this was the last straw. He demanded his release from the studio and forced them to pay him off. He left Hollywood, never worked for pictures again, and went to New York, where he did a show with Jimmy McHugh, *South American Way.*

"Al was a huge guy, 'way over six feet, and a little sloppy in the way he dressed. He looked like the foreman of a road gang, but he was really a very sensitive man, very well read and a great lyricist. He took offense easily. Berkeley once snubbed him on the set, and Al walked out and took a train for New York. They had to phone him to get the rest of the lyrics.

"We got along very well although we didn't socialize very much. He was a good audience for me, and we seldom had any problems. I remember telling him that the lyrics he had written for 'A Quarter to Nine' didn't fit the melody. He was incensed and stormed out, but he came back a couple of days later with a new set, and we used the other lyrics for 'Mammy, I'll Sing about You.'

"I didn't see much of him after he left Warners, and he died in New York in 1945."

HARD TO GET (1938)

For the remainder of Harry Warren's contract with Warners his lyricist was Johnny Mercer, with whom he would write several top songs. Their collaboration would fully establish Mercer

Busby Berkeley back in business, with his staging of "The Latin Quarter." Up front: Rudy Vallee, Rosemary Lane, Allen Jenkins and Mabel Todd.

Garden of the Moon: Johnny "Scat" Davis belts out "Love Is Where You Find It" as John Payne leads the band.

Garden of the Moon: "The Girlfriend of the Whirling Dervish" is none other than Jerry Colonna.

Garden of the Moon: A dishevelled Melville Cooper interupts Margaret Lindsay and Pat O'Brien.

as a songwriter of genuine style and originality. Their first hit was "You Must Have Been a Beautiful Baby," which is far and away the highlight of *Hard to Get*.

In this pedestrian comedy Dick Powell appears as a penniless but enterprising young businessman who tames a spoiled heiress, Olivia de Havilland. While taking her for a canoe ride on a lake, he sings the lilting song about the beautiful baby she must have been.

Warren and Mercer wrote one other song for this picture, "There's a Sunny Side to Every Situation," a cheery tune that is heard only in part when Powell hums and sings it to himself as he goes about his business around his gas station. The decision not to use it in full was a mistake—*Hard to Get* is a little hard to take, and another musical sequence would have helped.

Warren and Dubin were also required at this time to write a song for the Bette Davis picture *Jezebel*, but Max Steiner, who scored the film, objected to using the melody, and the song was used purely for exploitation. "Max didn't know about the song until he had almost completed scoring," says Warren, "and we didn't know he didn't know. It seldom occurred to the gentlemen in the front office that the creative people on their payroll were sensitive about such things."

Hard to Get was made early in 1938 and released in November. It was not a very productive year for Harry Warren because of a great tragedy that struck him and his wife in the spring—the death of their son, Harry. The boy was nineteen and a student musician. He was stricken with pneumonia, and no amount of care could save him. The death was a shattering blow to the Warrens, who closed their Beverly Hills home and moved to an apartment. Warren explains that the loss was a traumatic experience for his wife and that years would pass before the pain subsided. In a long life otherwise blessed with health and free of major problems, the death of their son remains the single calamity.

117

Hard to Get: Dick Powell singing "You Must Have Been a Beautiful Baby" to Olivia de Havilland.

GOING PLACES (1938)

Dick Powell's quest for better pictures began to look rather hopeless. *Hollywood Hotel* had been his high-water mark with big-budget musicals, and both *Cowboy from Brooklyn* and *Hard to Get* were steps downward. *Going Places* was a little better, but ironically its major song, "Jeepers Creepers," would be sung not by Powell, but by Louis Armstrong.

Warners had got plenty of mileage out of the Victor Mapes-William Collier play *The Hottentot*, and this was its fourth film version. Here Powell is a salesman for a sporting-goods store who poses as a famous gentleman jockey to promote business. He mingles with the horsy set and falls in love with Anita Louise, only to find himself trapped into riding her family's horse in a major race.

Comically, and improbably, he wins, despite his complete ignorance of horses. The horse he has to ride is named Jeepers Creepers, and it's a wild, spirited beast that can be calmed only by the singing of its groom, Louis Armstrong. In order for the horse to run the race Louis and his band have to mount a wagon and ride around the track, urging Jeepers on by singing its song.

The only love song in *Going Places* is "Say it with a Kiss," sung by Maxine Sullivan. Powell's warbling in this picture is limited to the comic patter "Oh, What a Horse Was Charley," sung in a hotel room with Walter Catlett, Harold Huber, and Allen Jenkins.

NAUGHTY BUT NICE (1939)

Dick Powell's last film for Warners, and his final association with Harry Warren, was a mild comedy in which he found himself taking second billing to Ann Sheridan. She was then being given a publicity campaign as "the Oomph Girl," and even though hers was a very limited singing voice, she sang more of the songs than Powell.

The original title was *The Professor Steps Out*, which tells more about it than *Naughty but Nice*. This time Powell, in quite a change of pace for him, is a music professor who goes to

Going Places: Dick Powell and Walter Catlett sing "Oh, What a Horse Was Charlie" to unimpressed Harold Huber and Allen Jenkins.

Going Places: Anita Louise and Dick Powell, and the horse they called "Jeepers Creepers," despite the name on the stall.

New York to try to get his symphony published. He gets mixed up with Tin Pan Alley types and forcefully becomes acquainted with the pop music styles of 1939. One such specimen is a clap-hands jive song danced and sung by Ann Sheridan:

The professor, a mild-mannered, bespectacled type, learns some of the facts of life about the music business, and *Naughty but Nice* is at its best when it satirizes the manner in which popular music feeds off classical compositions. Part of the plot hinges on a plagiarism case, and for this Warren had to write a melody that sounded as if it had come from a classic. As a pop song it's called "I Don't Believe in Signs," and to accommodate Sheridan's unusually low pitch, it had to be written in a key usually used by bass-baritones:

Of the five songs Warren and Mercer wrote for *Naughty but Nice*, none became hits beyond the run of the picture. The best of them is "In a Moment of Weakness," which Powell afterward recorded for Decca:

No other star introduced as many Harry Warren songs as Dick Powell, and yet, as Warren says, "Dick really wasn't that interested in being a singer. He liked it in the beginning, but he used to tell me he didn't think he was all that good, and I know that by the time we did this picture he was desperate to change his image. In time he became a good actor and director, and he had great luck in business.

"We didn't see much of each other after we left Warners, but when we did it was always friendly. He was quite a guy."

HONOLULU (1939)

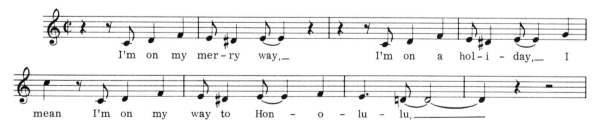

With so little musical activity on the Warners lot, the studio readily agreed to Harry Warren's going over to MGM to do a score for them. "I'm sure they were glad to get me off salary for a while," Harry says. "Gus Kahn was assigned to write the lyrics for the picture, and when they asked him who he wanted to do the music, he said me. We'd been friends for years, and it

Naughty But Nice: Dick Powell, as a bashful musicologist, listens to the artistry of his maiden aunts—Elizabeth Dunne, Vera Lewis and ZaSu Pitts, as they play an ancient air from the pen of Harry Warren.

Naughty But Nice: The musicologist is introduced to the world of the jitterbug. The young bandleader is Peter Lind Hayes.

was good to have a chance to do a picture with him. It was a nice job, maybe no great shakes as a movie but a pleasant one, and I had a good time doing it."

Honolulu stars Robert Young and Eleanor Powell, with George Burns and Gracie Allen lending comic support. Young appears in a dual role, as a movie star and a Hawaiian plantation owner, look-alikes with not a shade of difference. They decide to trade places for a while and find out what life is like in each other's shoes, and the star goes to Hawaii and falls in love with Eleanor.

Neither Young nor Powell sings any of the three Warren-Kahn songs. The sprightly title song makes for the perfect opener and closer, and as a background for the lovers we have:

The nearest thing to a production number in *Honolulu* is "The Leader Doesn't Like Music," with Gracie Allen impersonating Mae West and the King's Men, led by Ken Darby, as the Marx Brothers, with two of the King's Men as Groucho. The idea of the song, about a band leader with a peculiarity, might not make much sense, but it is a pleasing and tuneful bit of material:

After completing his work at MGM, Harry Warren returned to his office at Warners. The end of his contract was near, and neither he nor the studio had any plans to renew it. "Actually, we all thought the era of the musical was over," says Warren. "The whole thing had simmered down, and we figured the public had had enough. Of course, this turned out to be anything but the case, but none of us knew that early in 1939."

Warren's last job at Warners was writing a title song with Johnny Mercer for *Wings of the Navy*, one of the many pictures Hollywood made prior to the war to foster a greater appreciation of the armed services among Americans. This one, starring George Brent and John Payne, was a salute to the naval air service, and the song was a particularly good one, although it gained more popularity in England than in the United States. It was recorded by the band of the Grenadier Guards and for a time widely heard over the BBC:

About his departure from Warners, he says, "It was a strange, mixed feeling. I was eager to leave, but when you've worked somewhere for seven years you can't help feeling attached. I didn't like the bosses, but I'd made a lot of friends among the musicians; and I got cajoled into doing things I didn't like, like working on two pictures at the same time. What I did like was the fact that you couldn't turn on a radio in those days without hearing a song of mine, so maybe I should be grateful to Warners for having made me work so hard."

Almost all the Warner's musicals of the thirties were orchestrated by Ray Heindorf, who

122

On the set of *Naughty But Nice,* Ann Sheridan goes over a song with Malcolm Beelby, who was a mainstay of the Warners music department for all the years of the Warren-Berkeley-Powell musicals and long after.

In *Honolulu* Robert Young romances Eleanor Powell to the soft strains of Harry Warren's "This Night Was Made for Dreaming."

Honolulu: No. It isn't Mae West and the Marx Brothers. It's Gracie Allen and the King's Men: Bud Linn, Ken Darby, Rad Robinson and Jon Dodson, singing "The Leader Doesn't Like Music."

took over the direction of the music department when Leo Forbstein died in 1948. Few musicians have been as closely associated with motion pictures as Heindorf. He began playing piano accompaniments to silent pictures when he was fourteen, and he was a mere twenty-one when he orchestrated MGM's *The Hollywood Revue of 1929.*

Heindorf first met Harry Warren when Harry was on the staff of Shapiro, Bernstein and Company in New York in the late twenties, and from their working together at Warners came an abiding friendship. Says Heindorf, "It's hard to talk about Harry without sounding like a lush arrangement of one of his melodies. In the first place, the man is a genius, and secondly, you're never likely to meet a man who acts less like a genius. He was always an easygoing, sweet-natured man and maybe a bit too humble for his own good. If he'd had more ego and drive he would be a lot better known. But what he did have was this incredible gift for melody, and it was a constant amazement to all of us at Warners that he could turn out this stream of music with such ease. You can have all the musical education in the world and still not be able to write a good song. For that you need a melody—and that's the hardest thing to write, unless you happen to be Harry Warren. The real test for a melody is to play it with one finger on a piano. You can do that with his music, and it still sounds great."

In the opinion of Ray Heindorf, Harry Warren's somewhat dour view of working for Warners needs to be put in perspective: "Harry is a very sensitive man and easily hurt. In dealing with men like Jack Warner and Hal Wallis he was up against tough executives who ran that studio like a factory and turned out some great product. Music was only one of the many things they had to worry about.

"On the other hand, it was a great place for musicians because Warner liked music, and he gave Forbstein *carte blanche* in running that department. It was Warner who told Max Steiner that as far as he was concerned he could start his score with the main title and not stop until the end title. It was the same with Harry. Nobody told him what to write, and everybody at the studio, including Warner and Wallis, loved him."

124

A grouping of some of America's most prolific song writers at a party at the Trocadero in Hollywood in 1938: Al Dubin, Mack Gordon, Leo Robin, Harry Revel and Harry Warren, with Larry Hart and Hoagy Carmichael in front.

You're Getting to Be a Habit With Me

Words by
AL DUBIN

Music by
HARRY WARREN

I don't know ex-act-ly how it start-ed, But it start-ed in

fun;___ I just want-ed some-one to be gay with, To

* Symbols for Guitar and Banjo.

Copyright 1932 by M. Witmark & Sons. Copyright renewed.

Shadow Waltz

Words by
AL. DUBIN

Music by
HARRY WARREN

* Symbols for Guitar and Banjo

I Only Have Eyes For You

Lyric by
AL. DUBIN

Music by
HARRY WARREN

Diagrams for Guitar, Symbols for Ukulele and Banjo

Lullaby of Broadway

Lyric by
AL DUBIN

Music by
HARRY WARREN

* Symbols over Uke diagrams are for Tenor Banjo, Tenor Guitar and Six String Guitar

The rum-ble of a sub-way train,— The rat-tle of the tax-is.

The daf-fy-dils who en-ter-tain — at An-ge-lo's and Max-ie's. When a

Broad-way ba - by says "Good-night,"— It's ear-ly in the morn-ing.

Man-hat-tan ba - bies don't sleep tight — un - til the dawn;

'till ev - 'ry-thing gets ha - zy. "Hush - a - bye, I'll buy you

this and that," You hear a dad - dy say - ing.

And ba - by goes home to her flat to sleep all day.

Good - - night, Ba - - by.

About a Quarter to Nine

Lyric by
AL DUBIN

Music by
HARRY WARREN

*Symbols over Uke diagrams are for Tenor Banjo and Tenor Guitar.
**Symbols under Uke diagrams are for Six String Guitar

September in the Rain

Lyric by
AL DUBIN

Music by
HARRY WARREN

* *Symbols for Ukulele, Guitar and Banjo*

Remember Me?

Lyric by
AL DUBIN

Music by
HARRY WARREN

* *Symbols for Ukulele, Guitar and Banjo*

Jeepers Creepers

Lyric by
JOHNNY MERCER, *A.S.C.A.P.*

Music by
HARRY WARREN, *A.S.C.A.P.*

* *Diagrams for Guitar, Symbols for Ukulele and Banjo*

You Must Have Been a Beautiful Baby

Lyric by
JOHNNY MERCER, *A.S.C.A.P.*

Music by
HARRY WARREN, *A.S.C.A.P.*

PART THREE

GLORY DAYS AT FOX

Harry James, Mack Gordon, Glenn Miller, Harry Warren, and Sammy Kaye.

With Harry Warren, Busby Berkeley, and Dick Powell all leaving Warners at the same time, that studio's cycle of musicals came to an end as neatly as if it had all been planned to coincide with the end of the thirties. Warners would make musicals from time to time, but the genre would never again become a specialty with them. In the years to follow, the studios that geared themselves for the manufacture of musicals were Twentieth Century-Fox and Metro-Goldwyn-Mayer, with Harry Warren at one and then at the other.

Looking back to 1939, Warren says, "We had no idea there would be another cycle of musicals. In fact, it looked as if it was all over. I was on the verge of going back to New York, which I'd wanted to do ever since I got here, and write for the theater. Fate had other ideas. I got a call from Fox asking me if I'd like to write a score with Mack Gordon. I told them to discuss it with my agent, Vic Orsatti, and they made a deal."

Mack Gordon had been under contract to Paramount since 1933, when he and composer Harry Revel had written the songs for *Sitting Pretty*, which included "Did You Ever See a Dream Walking?" They moved to Fox in 1936 and became the Fox counterpart of Warners' Warren and Dubin, writing dozens of songs for the musicals of Shirley Temple and Alice Faye, among others.

Gordon and Revel first met in 1929, when Revel arrived in New York from England, looking for work as an entertainer. Gordon was a vaudeville actor, and the pair teamed as song-and-dance men on the circuits.

They began writing songs in 1931 and managed to place them in Broadway revues. However, by 1940 Revel and Gordon had had enough of each other's company and decided to end their partnership. In need of a composer, Gordon asked Darryl F. Zanuck if it would be possible to get Warren—an idea entirely to Zanuck's liking.

YOUNG PEOPLE (1940)

Harry Warren's first job at Fox—he was hired for just one picture, with no intimation of others—turned out to be Shirley Temple's swan song for the studio. After five years of great popularity, bringing in enormous revenue for Fox, she was now twelve years old and about to enter an awkward transition. *Young People* did little to arrest her decline. In this picture she appears as the adopted daughter of two vaudeville actors, Jack Oakie and Charlotte Greenwood, who must decide between continuing with their career, which includes the talented youngster, or retiring to give her a normal life. They decide upon life in the country and buy a farm in New England. The three of them are a happy family, and their love of life is expressed in a jolly song:

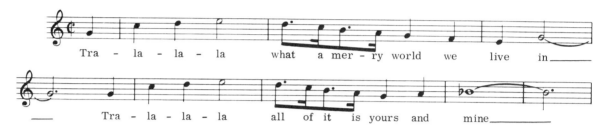

Tra - la - la - la what a mer - ry world we live in___
___ Tra - la - la - la all of it is yours and mine___

However, the joviality of Shirley, Oakie, and Greenwood is at variance with the rather dour nature of the local folk, who don't think much of show people, and the three find themselves treated coldly. All their attempts to win favor fall flat, and they eventually decide to quit life in the country.

Young People: Shirley Temple and Jack Oakie singing their way through a hurricane with the aid of a song by Harry Warren and Mack Gordon.

Young People: Jack Oakie, Shirley Temple and Charlotte Greenwood performing "On Fifth Avenue."

Just before their departure a severe rainstorm hits the area, and they reveal the kind of stamina and heroism the local people respect. Of course, they stay.

Young People uses a few clips from previous Shirley Temple pictures to establish her background as a child entertainer, and early in the picture she performs a song and dance, "Fifth Avenue," with Oakie and Greenwood. Of the three Warren-Gordon songs the one obviously couched in the Temple style was "I Wouldn't Take a Million":

DOWN ARGENTINA WAY (1940)

You'll find your life will be - gin ____ the ver - y mo - ment you're in ____ Ar - gen - ti - na ____ If you're ro - man - tic, Sen - or, ____ then you will sure - ly a - dore ____ Ar - gen - ti - na

The cycle of Hollywood wartime musicals began with *Down Argentina Way*. Although it appeared more than a year before U.S. entry into the war, the film was much more political than the public might have realized. The war in Europe had suddenly robbed Hollywood of a large segment of its market, and the anxiety-ridden moguls feared a decline in the industry. No such decline came; instead, the war years proved to be the glory days of Hollywood, a super-boom of popularity and profits for the picture people. Riding the crest of that boom were stars like Betty Grable and Alice Faye and songwriters Harry Warren and Mack Gordon.

To compensate for the loss of revenue from Europe—a situation that did not include the British Isles, where escapist movies like this were eagerly sought—the producers turned their attention to Latin America. That market had long been consistently good, but in late 1939 the producers decided to pay it much greater attention. Movie stars were sent on goodwill tours of South American cities and there was much talk of Pan-American unity. There was also a growing North American interest in Latin American dance music, owing in large measure to the dynamic Carmen Miranda.

Born in Portugal but raised in Rio de Janeiro, Miranda gained popularity while still a teen-ager, making hundreds of recordings and appearances in nightclubs. She was brought to New York in 1939 and given a leading role in the Broadway musical, *Streets of Paris*, the songs for which were written by Jimmy McHugh and Al Dubin and included "South American Way." Miranda made such an impression that her move to Hollywood was inevitable. She made her movie debut in *Down Argentina Way*, singing the McHugh-Dubin song, plus three of her own Brazilian specialties and the new material by Warren and Gordon.

Down Argentina Way was the film that put Betty Grable on the road to stardom. She had been in Hollywood since 1930, when she was fourteen, and had appeared in about thirty films. However, by 1940 she had almost despaired of success, and she left Hollywood to appear in the Cole Porter musical *DuBarry Was a Lady* on Broadway. This, as is often the case, rekindled the movie producers' interest, and when Alice Faye had to give up the lead in *Down Argentina Way* because of illness, it was offered to Grable. In time she would take over Faye's position as the top female star at Fox. Both women would dominate the Fox musical scene during the war years, and both would be very well served by Harry Warren. Of the fourteen Twentieth Century-Fox pictures for which he wrote music, ten featured Betty Grable and Alice Faye.

The plot of *Down Argentina Way* is paper thin. Grable is a New York heiress with a passion for racehorses, and Don Ameche is an Argentinian gentleman who brings some of his prize racers to the United States to sell. He and Grable fall in love, and she is invited to visit the family estate in the Argentine, accompanied by her high-kicking mother, Charlotte Greenwood. The delightful Greenwood is a little gutsy by local standards, and one of the high-lights of the picture is her duet with Leonid Kinskey, as a sly gentleman gigolo, of "Sing to Your Señorita."

Despite the silly story, the film has a pleasant and charming atmosphere, although the producers were criticized in Argentina for depicting life in that country falsely. Elsewhere there was little criticism, and moviegoers left the theaters humming the infectious melodies, including the very romantic ballad Ameche croons to Grable:

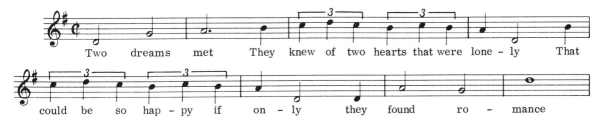

Two dreams met They knew of two hearts that were lone - ly That
could be so hap - py if on - ly they found ro - mance

Down Argentina Way: Betty Grable, Don Ameche and Henry Stephenson.

Down Argentina Way: Betty Grable doing the title song.

Down Argentina Way: Charlotte Greenwood and Leonid Kinskey performing "Sing to Your Senorita."

Down Argentina Way: Carmen Miranda and her boys.

TIN PAN ALLEY (1940)

Alice Faye spent her eleven years in the movies almost entirely at Twentieth Century–Fox, and six of her pictures, one after the other, featured music by Harry Warren. The first was *Tin Pan Alley*, which required only one new song to go along with a slew of standards from the era of the First World War.

The setting for this bright and breezy musical is the old music-publishing district of Manhattan, with Alice Faye and Betty Grable as singing sisters who become acquainted with song pluggers John Payne and Jack Oakie. Betty goes on to fame on the stage, and Alice opts for joining Payne and Oakie in their new and expanding publishing business, becoming their star plugger.

Briskly directed by Walter, the picture's hour and a half is packed with music, giving a spirited impression of the business with which it deals, and Warren and Gordon were assigned the job of selecting the songs used. Their own contribution, "You Say the Sweetest Things Baby," became instantly popular and remains Alice Faye's favorite song.

You say the sweet - est things, Ba - by, You have me rid - ing high.____

THAT NIGHT IN RIO (1941)

This song of love be - gins_____ the night they met down in Ri - o,

The success of *Down Argentina Way* made a wave of Latin American musicals inevitable. By now such Latin dance rhythms as the tango and the rumba had become widely popular in North America, and Carmen Miranda was in the vanguard of the movement.

Says Harry Warren, "Carmen was a fantastic woman, a really friendly, warmhearted female and a talented musician. She brought her own group from Brazil, and it was a joy to listen to them. They played with such vitality. Our fellows could play this music and make it sound good, but they didn't look as if they were enjoying it the way these Brazilian boys did. They had such humor and gusto."

Watching them inspired Warren to come up with some splendid Latin tunes. "I liked their music," he says, "and it wasn't hard to write for them once I mastered the rhythms. What made their music different was the rhythmic construction—the melodies were not all that different from ours. The rhythms fascinated me. They weren't Spanish like so much Latin American music—they were Portuguese mixed with native Brazilian strains—and it was a challenge to fit melodies to that beat."

That Night in Rio is conspicuous for Warren's fascination with Brazilian rhythms, beginning with Miranda and a large, lively group of dancers cavorting to "Chica, Chica, Boom Chic":

Come on and sing the Chic - a Chic - a Boom Chic,_____

That cra - zy thing, the Chic - a Chic - a Boom Chic,_____

Tin Pan Alley: Jack Oakie as the music publisher and Alice Faye as his song plugger. Their big hit, "You Say the Sweetest Things, Baby" is framed on the wall.

Tin Pan Alley: John Payne, Alice Faye and "You Say the Sweetest Things, Baby."

That Night in Rio: Alice Faye and Don Ameche.

That Night in Rio: Don Ameche and Leonid Kinskey listen while Alice Faye sings "They Met in Rio."

In *Down Argentina Way* Carmen Miranda had appeared as herself, but in this, her second film, the studio had discovered her pleasingly bizarre personality and allowed her to play a part. All her parts would be much the same, as a feisty bombshell, stunningly overdressed, and made up like a mad Kewpie doll, and fracturing the English language.

That Night in Rio is a handsome picture, with the rich Technicolor for which Fox musicals of this period were noted, and the screenplay is several cuts above the usual. It was based on the 1935 Maurice Chevalier picture *Folies Bergere* and contained enough sexual innuendoes for the censors to demand some deletions. Here Don Ameche plays dual roles, as an entertainer and as a business tycoon baron, with Alice Faye as the baroness and Miranda as the entertainer's jealous girlfriend. The complications are many, as the baroness hires the entertainer to impersonate her husband, to cover his absence at a conference, and later she can't be sure which man she is making love with.

Ultimately the four survive the various confusions and settle down with the right partners. It says much for the skill of Fox that all the plot ploys and a large amount of music neatly occupy a solid ninety minutes.

Neither Faye nor Ameche sings very much in *That Night in Rio*, mostly because the music was slanted toward Carmen Miranda but partly because some of their material was cut. The love song never became a hit, but it has a particularly beautiful melody:

Bo - a Noi - te moon - lit sky, Say good - night but not good - bye.

However, what truly lingers in the memory of *That Night in Rio* is the sight and sound of Carmen Miranda rolling her hips and her eyes and emitting a special brand of magic that only the most jaded could resist.

I, yi, yi, yi, yi, I like you ver - y much, I yi, yi, yi, yi, I think you're grand,_____ Why, why, why is it that when I feel your touch, My heart starts to beat, to beat the band._____

THE GREAT AMERICAN BROADCAST (1941)

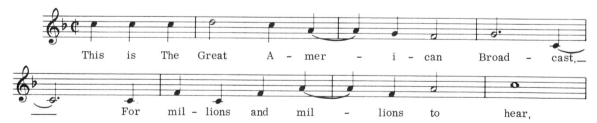

This is The Great A - mer - i - can Broad - cast,___ ___ For mil - lions and mil - lions to hear,

By now Harry Warren and Mack Gordon were the musical heroes of the Fox lot. The contract they had signed to do *Down Argentina Way* gave the studio the option to renew at the completion of the picture. Warren would come to regret this; however, at this point all parties were happy, and the public had come to expect Fox musicals to be full of good tunes.

174

The Great American Broadcast: Alice Faye singing "Where You Are" to John Payne.

The Great American Broadcast: Alice Faye and John Payne.

The Great American Broadcast: John Payne, Cesar Romero, Alice Faye and Jack Oakie.

The Great American Broadcast contains six Warren-Gordon songs, plus a fairly good yarn about the early days of radio. John Payne and Jack Oakie are the enterprising young men who see all kinds of opportunities after the First World War. Some of their schemes fail, but they make their mark in radio, broadcasting the Willard-Dempsey boxing bout in 1919.

Lending support is Alice Faye, as Payne's speakeasy-singer girlfriend. She becomes their chief attraction as they open their first radio station. One of her songs—carefully tailored by Warren and Gordon to fit the sultry Faye voice—is "Where You Are":

Where you are, that's where I want to be, For where you are is par - a - dise for me,

To fill out the story, the three protagonists run into misunderstandings, with Oakie and Payne parting company over business methods, and Faye, after her marriage, leaving Payne when he objects to her trying to raise money to save his failing station. She goes to New York and becomes a great success on radio, on a station owned by Oakie and his new partner, Cesar Romero. Romero hopes to win Alice, but he eventually realizes that she still loves Payne and helps to bring about a reconciliation.

The finale of the picture is the first great broadcast, a nationwide hookup of stations, with the film's stirring title song splendidly sung by baritone James Newill. Says Warren, "With this song I was trying to get a melody with a staccato beat, to approximate the tapping of the Morse code signals."

The finale of *The Great American Broadcast*, with performers wearing masks in the guise of famous broadcasters: Ben Bernie, Al Jolson, Rudy Vallee, Bing Crosby, Kate Smith, Eddie Cantor, Ted Lewis, Kay Kyser and Jimmie Fidler.

Viewed today *The Great American Broadcast* is even more interesting than in 1941, since it contains vignettes by such outstanding radio figures as Jack Benny, Walter Winchell, Rudy Vallee, Eddie Cantor, and Kate Smith, as well as valuable insight into the early days of radio in the United States.

The songs fit the picture beautifully, with Alice Faye getting the lion's share, as well she deserved. The catchiest of the songs is the rollicking "I Take to You," sung by Faye, Oakie, and Payne:

Like a duck takes to wa - ter,___ Like the flow - ers take to dew,___

___ Like a Lat - in takes to a La - tin Quar - ter,_ I take to you.___

What had been a one-shot assignment at the beginning had now developed into one of the great pairings in American songwriting, Harry Warren and Mack Gordon, who would emerge as the foremost musical team of the war years. Recalls Warren, "It took a while to get adjusted to Mack, because he was just about the opposite in temperament and life-style to me. He was a socializer, and he enjoyed the Hollywood life, going to parties with the producers and the stars. That didn't appeal to me at all. Working with him was similar to working with Dubin in that the ideas and most of the titles were his, and both of them would work from a lead sheet and come back with a complete set of lyrics.

"Dubin was the better-educated man, with a marvelous vocabulary. Mack didn't have the vocabulary, but he had an innate sense of song, and with his background as a performer he was a great demonstrator of material. What bothered me about working with him was his wanting to hear a melody over and over, until I was sick of hearing my own music. We got around this by hiring a pianist, and that way Mack could hear the stuff as much as he wanted after I had left the studio.

"I did most of my writing at the studio. We had our own bungalow, which was one of the joys of working at Fox, and in most cases I wrote the full melody of a song from the title or the main line of the lyrics. Some composers, like Richard Rodgers, like to write to the lyrics. To me that was always the hardest way of working."

SUN VALLEY SERENADE (1941)

It hap - pened___ in___ Sun__ Val - ley___

__ not__ so__ ver - y___ long__ a - go,

The idea for this pleasing musical came from a vacation Darryl F. Zanuck spent at the ski resort at Sun Valley, Idaho. He needed a vehicle for his famed skating star Sonja Henie, and in Sun Valley he found the perfect setting. It was also either his inspiration, or that of one of his employees, to hire Glenn Miller and his band, with the happy result that two of the four Warren-Gordon songs—"I Know Why" and "Chattanooga Choo Choo"—became smash hits.

Sun Valley Serenade: Sonja Henie.

Sun Valley Serenade: Sonja Henie and John Payne doing "The Kiss Polka."

Sun Valley Serenade: Glenn Miller, Sonja Henie and John Payne.

Actress Lynn Bari sings both "I Know Why" and the lilting title song, with some help from leading man John Payne. "Chattanooga Choo Choo" is a production number at the end of the picture, performed partly by the brilliant tap-dancing Nicholas Brothers.

Sonja Henie's appearances in previous films had been so limiting, requiring only her skating and her broad smile, that she was doubtful about continuing with a screen career. *Sun Valley Serenade* helped change her views, for in this film she got to play a rather saucy, spirited girl, and she showed a flair for comedy.

The plot starts out with the Miller band landing an engagement at Sun Valley and band pianist John Payne being stuck with responsibility for a Norwegian refugee, for whom he had vouched some months previously as a publicity gag. She turns out to be Sonja, very grateful and very romantically inclined. Payne at first rejects her but she finally gets him to reciprocate after they are marooned for a night in a mountain ski hut. Aiding the romance for publicity purposes is band manager Milton Berle.

The vivacious Sonja is a definite asset to *Sun Valley Serenade*, making its frothy Cinderella story seem plausible, and she is seen doing her speciality—skating in the resort's rink and starring in the elaborate production finale. The Miller band shines all through the picture, giving the music a feeling of quality and setting up several of the Warren melodies for instant approval.

Of the four songs, the least popular was "The Kiss Polka," although on screen it serves as an enjoyable dance sequence in the ski lodge and one of the few filmed occasions on which Sonja danced without skates.

Say, did you ev-er dance   The Kiss *(Kiss)*   Pol - ka? *(Kiss)(Kiss)*

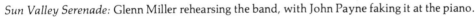

You can steal a kiss   to this *(Kiss)*   pol - ka, *(Kiss)(Kiss)*

So popular was the picture that another pairing of Glenn Miller and the music of Harry Warren was immediately agreed upon.

Sun Valley Serenade: Glenn Miller rehearsing the band, with John Payne faking it at the piano.

The city of Chattanooga, Tennessee, made Mack Gordon and Harry Warren honorary citizens for writing "Chattanooga Choo-Choo."

Dorothy Dandridge sings "Chattanooga Choo Choo" with the Nicholas Brothers in *Sun Valley Serenade*.

Sun Valley Serenade: The Nicholas Brothers dancing to "Chattanooga Choo-Choo."

WEEKEND IN HAVANA (1941)

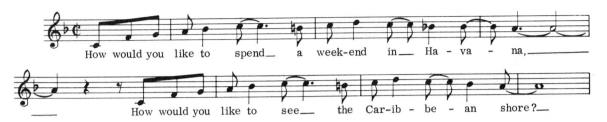

How would you like to spend__ a week-end in__ Ha - va - na,__

___ How would you like to see__ the Car-ib - be - an shore?__

John Payne was an actor with a very limited and ordinary singing voice and yet he became the number-one male star of Fox wartime musicals, seven of them with Warren music. His casting in these pictures pleased the songwriters less than it did the public, and yet his singing did nothing to stop the songs' becoming great favorites. Payne never recorded any of his songs, but neither did the other performers in Fox musicals of this period, except Carmen Miranda, whose career depended partly upon her recordings.

Darryl F. Zanuck was against his stars' making commercial recordings, feeling that the public would be more intrigued if they heard the stars only in movie theaters. It was a debatable point, not shared by most of the other studios. Even Alice Faye stopped recording her movie songs after 1937. This lack would become even more regrettable with time, when a later generation was to discover and appreciate the musicals of the Hollywood past and avidly collect material associated with them.

Week-end in Havana: John Payne, Alice Faye, Carmen Miranda and Cesar Romero.

Week-end in Havana: Carmen Miranda performing "When I Love, I Love."

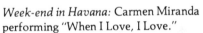

Admirers of Alice Faye believe that some of her best singing was done to the songs in the Warren scores and that the absence of recordings is disappointing, especially in the case of the lovely "Tropical Magic":

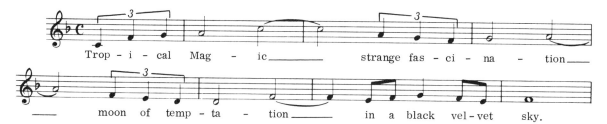

Weekend in Havana has a plot that almost defies summarizing. Alice plays a New York salesgirl on a vacation trip to Cuba, on a cruise ship that runs aground off Florida. She is flown to Havana by entertainer John Payne. There she is romanced by gambler Cesar Romero, to the chargrin of nightclub star Carmen Miranda, who keeps Romero as her manager despite his flighty ways. His only interest in Alice is that she might have money, which he needs to clear his debts. The complications include the arrival of Payne's fiancée from New York, but she might as well have saved her ticket. The inevitable outcome of such a picture is the pairing of Payne and Alice, and Romero's settling down with Carmen.

All of this takes place within a lively eighty-minute running time, with Walter Lang, an old hand at Fox musicals, directing. Greatly to the credit of this film is the rich Technicolor photography of Ernest Palmer, of a luster that has since gone from the screen.

Carmen Miranda has less music but more comedy in *Weekend in Havana* than in her earlier films. However, it was here that she sang "When I Love I Love," yet another Warren-Gordon song that would become a part of her unique repertory:

Harry Warren does not remember *Weekend in Havana* with fondness. He says, "They asked me to have all the music written in four weeks, because Carmen Miranda was leaving for another engagement. I worked nights as well as days and turned out a lot of music, some of which was dropped from the picture. I fell ill at this time and was taken to a hospital, where they found I had pnuemonia. It got worse, and I was on the critical list for some time.

"It was about three months before I returned to the studio. I found they had taken me off salary for the period of the illness but that they had kept Mack Gordon on all the time. I stormed into Zanuck's office, waving my walking stick and cursing, but they wouldn't let me see him. Maybe he didn't know anything about it, but his lieutenants did. They were horrible people. I demanded that my contract be terminated but they wouldn't do it, and my lawyer couldn't do anything about it either. I had to stay. But Fox didn't seem the same to me after that, and I was always looking for ways to get out."

ORCHESTRA WIVES (1942)

Orchestra Wives is one of the very few movies to give some insight into the lives of dance-band musicians on tour, and the light it sheds is fairly accurate. Glenn Miller here made his

Weekend in Havana: Alice Faye singing "Tropical Magic."

Weekend in Havana: Carmen Miranda singing the title song.

second, and unfortunately last, film appearance and performed reasonably well as an actor. He and his twenty-two-piece band, with George Montgomery as a trumpet player and Cesar Romero as a pianist, are seen making the rounds of one-nighters in endless dance halls.

In one such town a fan, Ann Rutherford, falls in love with Montgomery and marries him, but learns that the life of an orchestra wife is less than the round of enjoyment she had imagined. She joins the entourage of other wives, in the shapely forms of Carole Landis, Virginia Gilmore, and Mary Beth Hughes, and finds them to be a rather catty group, with far too much time on their hands for gossip. The main target for their speculations is the band's glamorous singer, Lynn Bari, whom they consider a *femme fatale* to their husbands.

Aside from the rift between the trumpet player and his bride, and their subsequent reconciliation, the film has no dramatic substance. However, it does have a generous amount of first-class music, splendidly played by Miller and his men, and if nothing else *Orchestra Wives* has the distinction of being the birthplace of three pop-song classics, "I Got a Gal in Kalamazoo," "At Last," and "Serenade in Blue."

All five of the Warren-Gordon songs for this picture were recorded by Glenn Miller, as well as by many other artists, "That's Sabotage," couched in jive rhythms, was a favorite of the day but seldom heard since, whereas "People Like You and Me" is kept alive by the Miller recording:

The love ballad from *Orchestra Wives* is not only pleasing in its languidly flowing tune, but unusual in containing subtle minor-mode phrasing not found in many popular songs of the war years:

The song about the gal in Kalamazoo, Michigan, caught the public fancy, even in England, where most people had no idea that a town with such a strange name even existed. Says Warren, "I had written the complete melody as a kind of rhythmic exercise, with no thought of

Orchestra Wives:
Glenn Miller and Cesar Romero.

An orchestra wife with a problem: Ann Rutherford finds her trumpeter husband, George Montgomery, in a hotel room with band singer Lynn Bari.

Orchestra Wives: Glenn Miller (center forward) and his orchestra playing "People Like You and Me," as Marian Hutton and the Modernaires sing it. Tex Beneke is at extreme right. That's Jackie Gleason at the left, Cesar Romero at the piano, and George Montgomery is in the back row.

lyrics, and Mack Gordon came up with this novel idea. He fitted his words to the music, and I've always thought that it was a very neat and clever piece of writing."

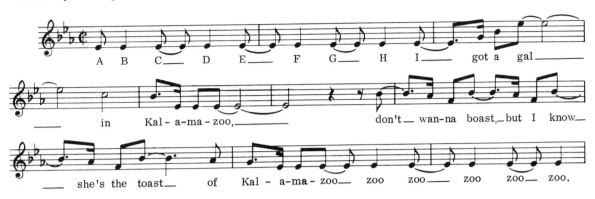

If "Serenade in Blue" had not become a standard it would probably be referred to as a "songwriter's song." It is a superior piece of music that allows for all manner of harmonizing, and Harry Warren credits Glenn Miller as the source of his inspiration. He says, "In writing songs for movies I had always cut my cloth to the performer and this was often a limiting factor. But I knew that Glenn could play anything I put on paper and that he would arrange the music in a way that could only enhance it. I liked him very much.

"Glenn was a gentle, quiet fellow and I never heard him raise his voice. And he was a master musician, more so than most people realize. I've heard him referred to as the Lawrence Welk of the war years, which is ridiculous. Miller not only created a beautiful, unique sound for his own band, but he had previously been the arranger for Ray Noble, the Dorseys, and many of the top bands. His influence was enormous. He was more responsible for the sound of the big-band era than anybody else.

"I wish I could have written more music for him but he went into the army right after this picture, and two years later he was dead."

ICELAND (1942)

The wartime musicals were rarely set in anything that could be described as reality. *Iceland* was unusual in being set on the North Atlantic island and its basic plot involved United States Marines stationed there. However, stars Sonja Henie, John Payne, and Jack Oakie never had to leave the Fox lot to make the picture.

Iceland: Sonja Henie and John Payne.

This was one of the first musicals made following U.S. entry into the war, and Harry Warren and Mack Gordon were naturally required to come up with a few songs to reflect the glowing spirit of patriotism. Two of the songs, "Let's Bring New Glory to Old Glory" and "I Like a Military Man," have long since faded into the background. So, too, has "You Can't Say No to a Soldier," but it is such a tuneful song that it remains in the memory of those who collect period music:

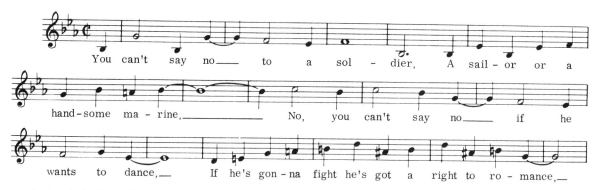

Iceland deals with the island only in the slightest way. In this very amusing film Payne is a marine who fancies himself a lady killer and is delighted to find the local girls so friendly. He

Iceland: Jack Oakie, John Payne and Sonja Henie getting acquainted to the tune of "It's the Lover's Knot."

Iceland: Jack Oakie, Joan Merrill, John Payne and Sonja Henie.

fails to reckon with the customs of his hosts, who consider brazen advances to be proposals rather than propositions.

Sonja and her family are eager for her to marry with the brash marine because it will allow the marriage of a younger daughter to a wealthy fish packer—by custom the older girl must marry first. Payne resists, and his breezy buddy Jack Oakie does his best to help, but after a while Payne is tamed and willing to settle down.

A complication arises when his American girl, singer Joan Merrill, arrives with Sammy Kaye and his band to entertain the troops, but she finally recognizes defeat.

Joan Merrill does most of the singing in this picture.

With Sonja Henie as its star, *Iceland* inevitably contains skating production numbers. How such expensive and expansive routines, involving tropical and Oriental settings, could be staged in a nightclub in Reykjavík is beyond explanation. The music is what matters, and one of the most enjoyable sequences is Warren's "Lover's Knot Polka," used at a party to announce engagements. But the song that shines from this film like a beacon is "There Will Never Be Another You." The melody, built on long rising and falling intervals, is one of the loveliest Warren ever wrote. For all its simplicity it is free of clichés and full of beguiling modulations. Like so many fine pieces of art, this song gives the impression of being written effortlessly. The notes follow each other with a gracious kind of logic.

Iceland: Joan Merrill singing "You Can't Say No to a Soldier," with Sammy Kaye and his Band.

SPRINGTIME IN THE ROCKIES (1942)

Since she appeared in *Down Argentina Way* Betty Grable's career had taken off like a rocket, and with the war years she would become one of the greatest assets in the history of Twentieth Century–Fox. In making *Springtime in the Rockies* the studio lined up the property with all the assurance of a crack shot aiming at a chicken at close range. Here they backed Grable with John Payne, Carmen Miranda, Cesar Romero, Harry James and his orchestra, and more songs by Warren and Gordon. All that, plus the lush brand of Fox Technicolor photography and stunning shots of the Canadian Rockies.

Any story would have carried this film to the bank. This one is yet another peek at the lives of show folks, with Grable and Payne as Broadway co-stars who love each other but can't get along. The picture opens with them in a theater singing and dancing to "Run, Little Raindrop, Run." The song had actually been written for *The Great American Broadcast* and cut, but wisely saved:

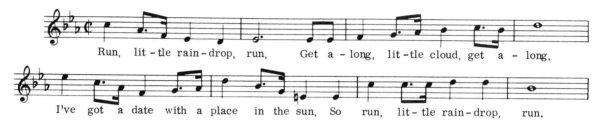

John Payne's problem in this musical is his roving eye, which offends Betty, so she takes off on a Western tour with her ex-partner, Cesar Romero. The jealous John follows and catches up with them at Lake Louise, Alberta—splendidly backdropped in the studio to save traveling costs. Payne's reclaiming Betty is, of course, purely a matter of time—the running time of the picture. Aiding him is his live-wire secretary, Carmen Miranda, who sings "Chattanooga Choo Choo" in Brazilian and a new one by Warren and Gordon:

Betty Grable was never more than an adequate singer, but such was the pleasing quality of her performance that moviegoers were hardly ever moved to criticize. She was, on the other hand, an excellent dancer, and in *Springtime in the Rockies* she has two fine dances with Cesar Romero, one of them the smooth ballroom melody "A Poem Set to Music" and the other the lavish finale, "Pan American Jubilee," with the whole cast sounding the message of unity throughout the Americas in a very agreeable manner:

The hit song from *Springtime in the Rockies* was "I Had the Craziest Dream," destined to become one of the most popular songs of the war years. The seductive melody was perfect for the trumpet of Harry James, and his recording, with singer Helen Forrest, was one of his major successes.

192

While working on this picture Betty Grable and Harry James began the romance that led to their marriage a few months later. The wedding caused some sighs of regret from multitudes of serviceman, who looked at their pinups of the luscious blonde and sang, "I want a girl just like the girl who married Harry James."

HELLO, FRISCO, HELLO (1943)

The ascendency of Betty Grable was partly due to Alice Faye's decision to end her career in favor of family life. While making *Weekend in Havana* she met and married bandleader Phil Harris and was off the screen for almost two years, during which she gave birth to her first daughter. She was still under contract to Fox, and she returned to make *Hello, Frisco, Hello* because legions of fans were still imploring the studio for more Faye pictures. They could hardly have been disappointed in *Hello, Frisco, Hello*, in which Faye looks more gorgeous than ever, singing turn-of-the-century songs in colorful costumes. Again John Payne and Jack Oakie are on hand in their familiar roles as lover and best friend.

Much of the picture is set in the entertainment emporiums of the Barbary Coast, resulting in an enormous amount of music. What little drama there is stems from Payne's dalliance with San Francisco society and the disappointed Alice's accepting an offer to star on the London stage. Payne's enterprises sink, but Alice subsidizes, through Oakie, his saloon-theater and makes a surprise appearance on stage at its reopening. The proud Payne swallows his pride and realizes where his true interests lie.

Springtime in the Rockies: Betty Grable and John Payne performing "Run, Little Raindrop, Run."

Springtime in the Rockies: Helen Forrest singing "I Had the Craziest Dream" with Harry James and his Orchestra.

Springtime in the Rockies: Cesar Romero and Betty Grable dancing to the "Pan American Jubilee."

Springtime in the Rockies: Betty Grable and John Payne, and a backdrop of Lake Louise.

Springtime in the Rockies: Betty Grable, John Payne, Carmen Miranda, Cesar Romero and Charlotte Greenwood, and the finale of "Pan American Jubilee."

The score of *Hello, Frisco, Hello* abounds with period songs and dances, although not all of them were actually written in the years of this plot. Only one new song was needed, to express Alice's feeling of unrequited love. Had this been an ordinary song it would doubtless have been lost in the sea of this film's music, but "You'll Never Know" was no ordinary song. It was instantly popular and within a few months became almost an anthem of the Second World War. Its winning an Oscar as the best song of the year was almost inevitable. It appeared on radio's "Your Hit Parade" for month after month.

"You'll Never Know" became Harry Warren's biggest success in terms of sheet-music sales, with over one million copies sold. "The song was a problem to write," he says, "because it had to serve two purposes. It had to fit into the period setting and sound like an old ballad, and yet we wanted to write a song that would express the feelings of all the war's separated lovers. Luckily we came up with something that managed to do just that. We didn't think too much about it until we happened to play it at a party and people immediately started to listen and sing it. It had that certain 'something' we all strive for.

"People often ask me if I know if I've written a hit. I don't. I've been crazy about some of my tunes, and yet they haven't caught on. When people would say to me, 'You'll have a big hit with that one,' I always thought of Verdi, whose reply was, 'We shall see.' The public decides what will be a hit."

SWEET ROSIE O'GRADY (1943)

Harry Warren's next assignment also turned out to be a period piece, although this time it would call for him to write several songs to fit the period, rather than to rely on old ones. *Sweet Rosie O'Grady* is very much a Grable vehicle, with no singing leading man to help, and the beauteous Betty cavorts through a half dozen routines.

The setting is New York in the 1880s, with Grable as a Brooklyn-born musical-comedy star who returns to the United States after great success on the English stage. Now known as Madeleine Marlowe and posing as a lady of refinement, she is taken to task by Robert Young, a reporter for the *Police Gazette*. She has to admit to her past as Rosie O'Grady, who started out as a singer on the Bowery, but she turns the tables on Young by charging that he is a former suitor trying to further his career with publicity. One of her tricks is to bedeck a whole line of chorus boys with masks of Young, called Sam Magee in the picture, and from this comes the song "My Sam."

She also performs several routines in her role as a theater star, including "Get Your Police Gazette," "The Wishing Waltz," "Where, Oh Where, Is the Groom?" and the jaunty "Goin' to the County Fair":

Snap your tie on and slick your hair,— We got-ta git-a-go-in' to the coun-ty fair.—

Fetch the bug-gy and hitch the mare— We got-ta-git-a go-in' to the coun-ty fair.—

According to Harry Warren, Betty Grable was an easy performer to work with. "I don't remember her ever objecting to a song or causing any problems," he says. "When I first knew her she was very friendly. She cooled a little with time, as they all do, and became a bit remote. From what I could see of it, there wasn't anything easy about being a star."

Mack Gordon, Alice Faye and Harry Warren on the set of *Hello, Frisco, Hello*.

Sweet Rosie O'Grady: Betty Grable singing "My Heart Tells Me" in the bathtub.

Hello, Frisco, Hello: Alice Faye singing "You'll Never Know."

Sweet Rosie O'Grady is a choice item for Grable fans, allowing her to perform a generous amount of material in a pleasing, vivacious manner. She had a good sense of humor, and that quality is in abundance in this picture. She was, of course, surrounded by Fox expertise, by creative designers and photographers, and especially well backed by the superb Fox music department under the direction of Alfred Newman. The dance director was Hermes Pan, who was responsible for most of the dancing in the Fox wartime musicals. Pan might not have had the cinematic imagination of Busby Berkeley, but he was an elegant and tasteful dance

Sweet Rosie O'Grady: Betty Grable singing "My Heart Tells Me."

director. He was also a performer in his own right, and he dances with Grable in one of the production numbers of this film. However, perhaps the one lingering memory of *Sweet Rosie O'Grady* is the simple scene in which Betty Grable sits in a bathtub singing the picture's most popular song, "My Heart Tells Me":

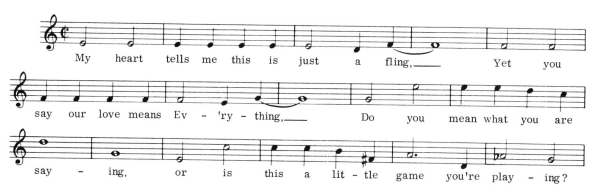

My heart tells me this is just a fling,____ Yet you say our love means Ev - 'ry - thing,____ Do you mean what you are say - ing, or is this a lit - tle game you're play - ing?

THE GANG'S ALL HERE (1943)

The Gang's All Here was Alice Faye's last movie musical and Harry Warren's biggest score at Fox, with eleven songs written and three dropped. It was his first Fox picture with a lyricist other than Mack Gordon. Gordon was anxious to become a producer and decided to pass up this assignment and concentrate on production plans.

Leo Robin was hired as the lyricist, which was the start of an agreeable association. Says Warren, "Leo is such a gentleman that I've always thought of him as the Mary Pickford of lyricists."

The Gang's All Here is especially notable for being Busby Berkeley's first film in color and his best job as a director. Berkeley had been working at MGM since leaving Warners in 1939, and Fox made an arrangement to get him for this project. A common opinion in Hollywood was that it was regrettable that none of the Warner musicals had been in color, to get the full value of Berkeley's weird and wonderful fantasies. This picture proves what Berkeley could do with the addition of color. Unfortunately, it came at a bad time in his life, when his personal affairs were leading him to a nervous breakdown and the loss of his finances. He would never again reach these heights or get an opportunity like this one.

The Gang's All Here has plenty of musical sequences but a pitifully thin story. Looking at the script, Harry Warren thought he had been sent back to Warners and back in time, a feeling accentuated by working once more with "Mad Buzz." Alice Faye was pregnant with her second child, and she lacked much of her former sparkle. That lack might have come from reading the script.

Here she portrays a singer in a New York nightclub, pestered by a handsome sergeant, James Ellison, who manages to win her love but fails to tell her he is the scion of a wealthy family and engaged to the daughter of another rich family. He goes overseas, and when he returns, his father invites the whole theatrical troupe, plus Benny Goodman's band, to stage a show on his estate. Romantic and comedic misunderstandings rise from this situation, but it happily evolves that Ellison's fiancée, Sheila Ryan, is more interested in a theatrical career than in him and accepts an offer to become a dancing partner of Tony DeMarco.

Fox had the same problem with Berkeley as had Warners—restraining him. The picture runs longer than most Fox musicals, going a little beyond a hundred minutes, but almost half of that

198

Sweet Rosie O'Grady: Betty Grable performing "Going to the County Fair."

Sweet Rosie O'Grady: Betty Grable and Robert Young.

is devoted to music. It opens in a nightclub, with a number built around the arrival of a ship from South America carrying Carmen Miranda and hordes of excited passengers:

You're in the kind of a place that seems like a lit-tle cab-a-ret in Ri-o, Then you hear a boo-gie woo-gie tri-o, And you dis-cov-er you're in New York,

The opening number is a whirling-dervish affair with Berkeley using a camera crane to swoop in and out among the dancers. This frenzy is nothing compared to "The Lady in the Tutti-Frutti Hat," with Carmen Miranda at a tropical-fruit plantation and a vast number of girls dancing with huge bananas. This routine was excised from prints shown in Latin America, where it was looked upon as vulgar. Viewed today it certainly is open to Freudian interpretation, but as Warren recalls, "Our concern at the time was length. Buzz was back to his old tricks. It went on and on and on. He never knew when to stop. I got so tired of hearing the Tutti-Frutti melody that I wrote another one to give the arrangement some relief. Sometime later I gave it to lyricist Bob Russell, and we made it into a song called 'Carnival.' "

Heard the sound of laugh-ter And saw the mis-sion gates o-pen'd wide, Saw her sell-ing kiss-es That ca-bal-ler-os bought star-ry eyed;

The Gang's All Here: Alice Faye sings "A Journey to a Star" to James Ellison.

The Gang's All Here: Carmen Miranda and the beginning of "The Lady in the Tutti-Frutti Hat" number.

The Gang's All Here: More of "The Lady in the Tutti-Frutti Hat." The girls with their gigantic bananas struck some people as being strangely vulgar.

The two best songs in *The Gang's All Here* are both crooned by Alice Faye. One has a definite wartime feeling in its lyrics:

No love, no noth - in', _____ Un - til my ba - by comes home. _
_____ No, Sir! No noth-in', ___ As long as ba - by must roam, _

Alice sings "No Love, No Nothin' " to a photo of her overseas lover, but before he leaves she sings "A Journey to a Star" directly to him on the Staten Island ferry. She tells him it is a song for her new show, although the sergeant is too love stricken to appreciate the quality of the music:

A jour - ney to a star _ would not be ver-y far _ As long as I'm a-lone _ with you.

Benny Goodman and his band are also much in evidence in *The Gang's All Here*. Warren and Robin supplied two songs written in a typical Goodman swing style, "Minnie's in the Money," which is marked by a now-dated wartime connotation, and a piece with remarkable rhythmic accents:

Pa - du - cah, _____ Pa - du - cah, _____ If you wan-na you can rhyme it with ba-
zoo-ka, But you can't pooh pooh Pa-du - cah, That's an - oth-er name for Par - a-dise.

The Gang's All Here: Tony De Marco and Carmen Miranda doing "Paducah."

The Gang's All Here: Sheila Ryan and Tony De Marco dance to Benny Goodman and his orchestra, while Phil Baker, Carmen Miranda, Alice Faye and Charlotte Greenwood look on.

The film's ending is Berkeley at his best. The song "The Polka Dot Polka" is charmingly sung by Alice and a group of children in the costumes of various periods, but then it expands into a lavish and fantastic surrealistic ballet, with Berkeley photographing his girls in kaleidoscopic formations and with trick color effects.

Like the hat Miranda wears in her Tutti-Frutti number, *The Gang's All Here* is a bit much, and yet for anyone interested in the art of movie musicals it is required viewing. Composer Warren says, "I never saw it. It was bad enough having to work on it."

BILLY ROSE'S DIAMOND HORSESHOE (1945)

Twentieth Century-Fox paid Billy Rose seventy-six thousand dollars for his concept of a musical built around his New York nightclub and then discovered that he wouldn't let them release it unless his name was part of the title. Filmed in mid-1944, the picture was delayed until April 1945 while the Fox lawyers tried to persuade Rose to back down. He didn't, and he even insisted that theater marquees spell out the title in full.

This was of some amusement and satisfaction to Harry Warren, who says, "Having known Billy for a long time, I knew that was the stand he would take. I didn't care much for the title, but I despised the Fox lawyers so much that I enjoyed seeing Billy get away with it.

"The Hollywood lawyer is a special breed of cat, and I have nothing good to say about him. These people ruined my stay at Fox with their legal tricks. Their complicated language confused me, and after signing my contract I discovered that Twentieth Century–Fox was legally the author of my music. This gave them control of the music and half of the royalties coming to myself and the lyricist.

"I had been trying to get out of the contract for a long time, and after *The Gang's All Here* they let me go because they had no musicals lined up. Alice had left, and Betty was off the screen for a year having a baby.

"I signed with MGM in early 1944 but came back to Fox soon afterward to do this picture because Billy Rose asked that I do the music. I imagine Betty might also have had something to do with it—she was a very shrewd girl, a real pro."

Billy Rose's Diamond Horseshoe:
Betty Grable and friends doing the
"Cooking Up a Show" number.

Billy Rose's Diamond Horseshoe was a big-budget musical, and Fox undoubtedly wanted to assure its success with songs by Warren and Gordon. Warren had his own lawyer check the contract to make sure it was a purely one-picture deal, and then proceeded to write music that in no way reflected any of the resentment he felt about Fox.

The score is big and includes several old numbers by other writers in addition to the six new Warren-Gordon songs. The script is also the best of any of the Fox musicals with which Warren was associated. It was written by George Seaton—this was also his first assignment as a director—who adapted it from the old play *The Barker*, by John Kenyon Nicholson.

In this very pleasing musical Grable is the top-lined entertainer of the Diamond Horseshoe, owned and managed by William Gaxton, himself a performer. The picture opens with Gaxton and his players performing an elaborate production number, "Putting on a Show." The nightclub is the scene of most of the film's music, which includes a jam-session dance, "A Nickel's Worth of Jive," and a spirited Latin song and dance, "In Acapulco," with Grable doing what Carmen Miranda would have done had she been available and not working on another picture:

If you're ro-man-tic, chum,_ Pack up your duds and come_ to A-ca-pul - co._____

_____ You put your cares in hock_and throw a-way your clock_ in A-ca-pul - co._

Dick Haymes received his first starring role in *Billy Rose's Diamond Horseshoe*. He was popular because of his singing with Tommy Dorsey's band, and Fox decided to give him star treatment. Haymes would not prove a good film investment, but as a singer he would acquire an enviable reputation. Says Warren, "With the exception of Crosby, Haymes was the best of the popular singers, including Sinatra. Dick couldn't handle a rhythm song as well as Frank, but I like what he did with ballads better."

Billy Rose's Diamond Horseshoe: Beatrice Kay, William Gaxton and Betty Grable doing "A Nickel's Worth of Jive."

Billy Rose's Diamond Horseshoe: Betty Grable "In Acapulco."

The big ballad from this picture was "The More I See You," and the Haymes recording was a smash hit in 1945. His role here is that of the medical-student son of William Gaxton, who doesn't want the boy to become a part of show business. The boy, on the other hand, has a liking for the business and once he falls in love with Grable he is ready to forget medicine.

She gets blamed for his defection, but in the end it is Betty who puts Dick back on the road to becoming a doctor, as well as winning his heart.

Phil Silvers is also on hand as a frantic stage manager, and Beatrice Kay, who specialized in ballads of the Gay Nineties, does some old songs, with a lead-in song, "Play Me an Old-Fashioned Melody," by Warren and Gordon.

But is the ballads from *Billy Rose's Diamond Horseshoe* that linger in the memory, Haymes singing "The More I See You" and Grable quietly crooning another one almost as good:

I wish I knew some-one like you could love me,
I wish I knew you place no one a-bove me,

Harry Warren's last song for Twentieth Century–Fox brought him no money at all. Mack Gordon, ever ambitious to become a film producer, finally got a go-ahead from Zanuck to produce a musical called *Three Little Girls in Blue,* with Vera-Ellen, Vivian Blaine, and June

Billy Rose's Diamond Horseshoe: Dick Haymes singing "The More I See You."

Haver in the title roles. Gordon hired composer Joseph Myrow to write the score, since Warren was no longer willing to work for Fox, but for sentimental reasons he asked Warren to write one song with him. "This Is Always" turned out to be the one song cut in the final editing of the picture:

This is-n't some-times, this is al - ways. This is-n't may-be, this is al - ways.

In negotiating a price for the song, Warren decided that instead of money he would ask for several prints of the Fox musicals for which he had written. This was a verbal agreement with executive Lew Schreiber, but Schreiber died shortly afterward, and Warren never received the prints.

Looking back on his four years at Twentieth Century-Fox, Warren says, "Yes, they were great years for the picture business, and we were able to come up with some good songs, but my recollections include many bitter moments with movie executives and their lawyers. They were hard people, and I could never understand them. They would talk millions, and yet they would haggle over a few cents' more royalties on copies of songs. We never could get them to increase the royalty rates.

"I remember when we did the first Glenn Miller picture and the songs were getting a tremendous play, we received what seemed like a very small statement. Mack and I stormed into the legal department for an explanation. The lawyer chuckled, 'You didn't read your contract, did you?' Then we found out that the publishers were getting fifty percent of the royalties, and Fox was taking another twenty-five, with the remainder split between Mack and myself. I think what really annoyed us was the glee this lawyer seemed to take in making us feel we had been suckered, as if it was all some great big game."

Billy Rose's Diamond Horseshoe: Carmen Cavallaro accompanies Betty Grable as she sings "I Wish I Knew."

In comparing his Warner period with his Fox period, Warren agrees that the general standard of the pictures was better during the war years and that the feeling of confidence made it an exciting time. "I think my music at Fox was better than what I had done previously. In my opinion, the more you write the better you get—and I hadn't stopped writing since I arrived in Hollywood in 1932. When I left Fox I still thought I might get back to New York and write for the theater, but the fates pinned me down in Hollywood."

During the years at Fox, Warren became closely associated with Herbert Spencer, one of the industry's top arrangers and orchestrators. Spencer was responsible for arranging many of Warren's songs in this period and he says: "There are some things that sheer labor won't produce, and one of them is inspired melody. As an orchestrator you acquire a sixth sense about how a composer has arrived at his product. The strain is sometimes very apparent—the music comes to you almost smelling of perspiration. It was never this way with Harry's melodies. I'm sure he had to dig to get them, but they were so logical in their lines and developments they sounded as if they had written themselves. There's no explanation for this. It smacks of the divine, and I have often wondered if Harry himself realized it. Working with him was a pleasure because, aside from his being a very warm and humorous man, he was always there to discuss his music with the arrangers. This was not the case with men like Irving Berlin and Cole Porter, who turned in their sketches and left. Harry seemed to write with orchestration in mind and if we did well by his music it was because we had him on hand to work with—and he was *simpatico*. That's the word that best fits Harry Warren in my mind—*simpatico*—musically and personally."

I Had the Craziest Dream

Words by
MACK GORDON
A.S.C.A.P.

Music by
HARRY WARREN
A.S.C.A.P.

I Know Why (And So Do You)

Lyric by
MACK GORDON

Music by
HARRY WARREN

Chattanooga Choo Choo

Lyric by
MACK GORDON

Music by
HARRY WARREN

7302-4

She's gon-na cry _____ un-til I tell her that I'll nev-er roam, _____

So Chat-ta-noo-ga Choo-Choo won't_ you choo-choo me home. _____

Chat-ta-noo-ga Choo-Choo won't

_ you choo - choo me home. _____

7302-4

There Will Never Be Another You

Words by
MACK GORDON
A.S.C.A.P.

Music by
HARRY WARREN
A.S.C.A.P.

Serenade in Blue

Words by
MACK GORDON
A.S.C.A.P.

Music by
HARRY WARREN
A.S.C.A.P.

Slow Blues Tempo

When I hear that Ser-e-nade In Blue, ———— I'm some-where In an oth-er world a-

lone with you, shar-ing all the joys we used to know, ——— man-y moons

— a - go. Once a-gain your face comes back to me, ———— just

The More I See You

Words by
MACK GORDON
a.s.c.a.p.

Music by
HARRY WARREN
a.s.c.a.p.

You'll Never Know

Words by
MACK GORDON
A.S.C.A.P.

Music by
HARRY WARREN
A.S.C.A.P.

Copyright 1943 by Twentieth Century Music Corporation. Renewed 1970.

PART FOUR

METRO AT LAST

Harry Warren, signing his MGM contract with Louis B. Mayer, as Loews' Vice President Charles Moscowitz looks on.

Harry Warren got his contract with Metro-Goldwyn-Mayer entirely because of Arthur Freed, who had told him as far back as 1941 that the moment he was clear of his Fox commitments an office would be waiting for him at Metro. It may have been irritating to Warren at the time that Fox exercised its options on his contract, but it was to his good in retrospect, because the Fox musicals produced more Warren standards than would his years with MGM, the foremost producer of movie musicals. And no one in 1944 could have predicted that musicals were in their last major phase.

The high standards of musicals at Metro were largely due to the man who ran the studio, Louis B. Mayer. Says Warren, "Mayer has been much maligned as a tyrant and ridiculed because of his emotional temperament. I don't go along with all this. Of all the moguls I had any dealings with, Mayer was the most courteous and considerate. He loved music, and the people he seemed to like best were composers, musicians, and singers. When he hired Johnny Green as the director of the music department, he told him he wanted the greatest orchestra and arrangers in the business. Johnny pointed out that it would cost a lot of money, and Mayer said, 'We've got a lot of money.' Working for Mayer was a pleasure, and he also paid me more than anyone else."

For the amusement of his fellow songwriters, Warren wrote a piece that conveyed his feelings about working at the various studios. The section dealing with Warners is agitato, giving the feeling of machinery at full tilt, and the lyrics refer to prison guards walking the walls and spying on the inmates. The section for Metro is pastorale and includes the line "The birds sing all day long." The song has meaning only for those who have worked in Hollywood, but it is typical of Warren's dry sense of humor. Warren's quips about Hollywood people are pungent and tend to sound snide when taken out of context. Invariably they are affectionate ribbings of people he likes.

Aside from the munificent attitude of Louis B. Mayer toward music, the Metro musical gathered most of its momentum and esteem from Arthur Freed. The studio had produced musicals all through the thirties; in fact lyricist Freed and composer Nacio Herb Brown had written the songs for the first Metro musical, *The Broadway Melody* produced in 1929, which included "Singin' in the Rain" and was the precursor of the *Broadway Melody* series. But not until Freed became a producer for MGM in 1939 did they start to turn out the product that would be identifiable as "an MGM musical." Freed was partly responsible for *The Wizard of Oz*, and his first complete production was *Babes in Arms*, starring Judy Garland and Mickey Rooney and directed by Busby Berkeley. Over the next twenty years would come a remarkable string of more than forty musicals, the very finest of their genre.

Warren says, "Freed was the greatest producer of musicals because he loved them and because he was himself a songwriter. It was a case of the right man in the right place at the right time. He had told me for years that he wanted to work with me as a writer, but the circumstances were never right. When he became a producer at Metro I was locked in by Fox, but when I was free he couldn't get me there fast enough.

"Arthur gave me an office next to his in the Thalberg building, but I had to move out because there was just too much activity, with everybody and his dog dropping in. He then gave me a bungalow on the lot, and it was a perfect arrangement. Nobody bothered me or told me what I could or couldn't do. Arthur was a marvelous guy to work for. Most of the time he was placid and easygoing, but he had occasional fits of frightening temper. He could be tough."

ZIEGFELD FOLLIES (1946)

Ziegfeld Follies was begun in 1944 and released two years later, with much of that time spent in production. It remains the most fantastic of all Metro musicals, and according to Harry Warren, enough material was shot to make a second picture. The film has no plot, other than an opening in which William Powell, as Florenz Ziegfeld in heaven, muses about a show he

Ziegfeld Follies: Lucille Bremer and Fred Astaire dancing to "This Heart of Mine."

Ziegfeld Follies.

could do if all the MGM talent were available to him. This triggers a revue of gargantuan proportions, such as will probably never be seen again in a Hollywood movie.

Running two minutes short of two hours long, *Ziegfeld Follies* consists of twelve segments, each running eight to ten minutes, in which stars such as Lucille Ball, Esther Williams, Fred Astaire, Lena Horne, Fanny Brice, Red Skelton, Gene Kelly, and Kathryn Grayson perform a variety of musical and comedic material. Harry Warren's contributions, with lyrics by Arthur Freed, are "This Heart of Mine," which would become a standard, and "There's Beauty Everywhere." The latter is used as the finale, with Kathryn Grayson singing the song in a bizarre, surrealistic setting of colored shapes and bubbles. Originally the song was planned for James Melton, but the producers changed their minds and gave it to Grayson, whom they considered a much better bet for stardom. This displeased Melton, but he was instead given an aria from Verdi's *La Traviata*.

There's beau - ty ev - 'ry - where,___ That ev - 'ry - one can share;

Of all the stars performing in *Ziegfeld Follies* Fred Astaire emerges with most of the best material. He talks about Ziegfeld at the beginning of the picture and dances in three segments—the memorable dance duet with Gene Kelly, "The Babbitt and the Bromide," the dramatic ballet "Limehouse Blues," with Lucille Bremer, and a dance story built around the song "This Heart of Mine," also with Bremer.

Vincente Minnelli received sole credit for directing this picture, although various segments were done by other directors. However, "This Heart of Mine" is Minnelli's work and greatly to his credit. The choreographer was Robert Alton. The sequence takes place in a ballroom, with Astaire as a gentleman jewel thief, a la Raffles, who courts Lucille Bremer with the object of robbing her. He first sings the song to her in his soft, charming manner as they dance, and then with cinematic license the ballroom becomes isolated and much more unreal in its splendor, as the couple whirls to Warren's very romantic melody. Astaire succeeds in his robbery, but Bremer realizes his game and willingly offers the rest of her jewels and herself. As a song "This Heart of Mine" is pleasing, but as the basis for this elegant dance it is enchanting.

YOLANDA AND THE THIEF (1945)

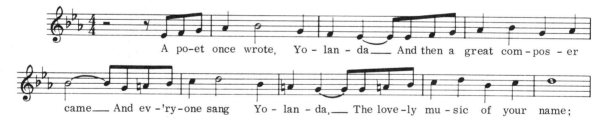

A po-et once wrote, Yo - lan - da___ And then a great com - pos - er came___ And ev - 'ry-one sang Yo - lan - da,___ The love-ly mu - sic of your name;

With Fred Astaire again a thief and Lucille Bremer as the rich young girl he tries to rob, audiences might well have considered *Yolanda and the Thief* an extension of the "This Heart of Mine" sequence in *Ziegfeld Follies*. The similarity was purely a coincidence. The Irving Brecher screenplay was based on a story by Ludwig Bemelmans and Jacques Thery, with the fanciful Bemelmans touch the key ingredient.

Ziegfeld Follies: Kathryn Grayson singing "There's Beauty Everywhere."

This picture is a fantasy but with a quaintness that did not appeal to the mass of moviegoers in 1945. The setting is Latin American and very Catholic, with Astaire as a con man–crooked gambler who pretends to be the materialized guardian angel of Bremer, a superwealthy heiress and an extremely gullible young beauty. Casting Lucille Bremer was a mistake, since she gave the impression of being more worldly than the part required. A young Audrey Hepburn would have been perfect. Producer Arthur Freed assigned himself as the lyricist, which was also a mistake. The film needed a much more elegant and poetic touch.

The five Warren-Freed songs for *Yolanda and the Thief* serve to help tell the story, and none of them became popular away from the picture. The first one, "This Is the Day for Love," is sung by Yolanda and the girls at the convent to which she belongs. Later, Astaire overhears Yolanda praying to her guardian angel in the garden of her aunt's home. She sings "Angel" to herself, and he decides to take advantage of the situation, presenting himself to her in her lulled and dreamy state. To further charm her he sings "Yolanda," accompanying himself on the harp to strengthen his heavenly appearance and following it with a beguiling dance. This all leads to the inevitable conclusion—Astaire and Bremer fall in love, and he is unable to go through with his crooked plans.

His anxieties and desires are shown in a dream sequence built around the song "Will You Marry Me?" In this surreal and darkly erotic ballet Astaire is torn between his dishonesty and

235

his growing love for the girl. The film ends on a much happier theme with "Coffee Time," an energetic Latin song and dance in a carnival setting in which Astaire and Bremer express an exhilarating feeling of relief and joy. It is also a good choice for the finale because as a tune this was the one the audiences would most likely hum on the way out of the theater:

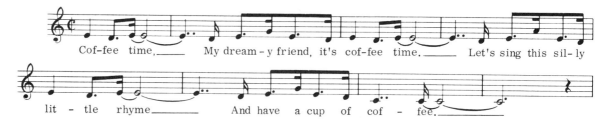

Cof-fee time,____ My dream-y friend, it's cof-fee time.____ Let's sing this sil-ly
lit - tle rhyme_____ And have a cup of cof - fee.____

Yolanda and the Thief might not have pleased the public, but it remains a prime example of the skill and artistry of Metro's group of film-musical experts. Director Vincente Minnelli had begun his career as an art director, and his taste and imagination are beautifully apparent here. So, too, is the Technicolor photography of Charles Rosher and the costumes of Irene Sharaff. Lennie Hayton was the music director and Conrad Salinger the orchestrator. These were all names that appeared on the credits of MGM musicals throughout the forties and early fifties, contributing to a unique chapter in film history.

The film's failure was a keen disappointment for Harry Warren, since it was the kind of vehicle he had long wanted to work on. He says, "Ever since I'd been in Hollywood I'd been deploring the feeble scripts of most of the musicals I had done, even though they had resulted in lots of hit songs. I loved the script of *Yolanda*, and we all thought we would come up with a winner. But fantasy is the hardest thing to put on the screen; seeing it in your mind's eye when you read it and then making it come alive is terribly difficult. The end result was less than what we aimed for, but I still think the picture is charming, and it's the kind of project that really interests me as a composer."

Yolanda and the Thief: Lucille Bremer, after being serenaded by little girls singing "This Is the Day for Love," is approached by con man Fred Astaire.

THE HARVEY GIRLS (1946)

The kind of success Harry Warren had been hoping for in joining MGM came with *The Harvey Girls,* an expensive vehicle designed for Judy Garland in her peak period. The idea for the film was particularly good, telling the story of Fred Harvey's chain of restaurants, which followed the railroad westward, and how he staffed them with waitresses. Harvey's standards of decorum and cleanliness were high, but the film fictionalizes his girls as paragons of virtue, in contrast to the rough men and wild women of the Western frontier.

The Freed unit, by now the elite corps at Metro, brought all their plentiful resources to bear, with Lennie Hayton again the music director and Conrad Salinger the orchestrator. Freed was far too busy to attempt the lyrics and asked Warren whom he would like to have do them. Warren thought the best man for the job was Johnny Mercer, since it called for his brand of Americana. (Alistair Cooke described Mercer's lyrics as being "little bits of Mark Twain.")

This film also, in Harry Warren's opinion, benefited greatly from Freed's choice of director. "George Sidney was marvelous because he loved music. He'd been at MGM since he was a teenager, and he'd always collected records and sheet music and instruments. He was almost good enough to have been a professional musician. It's a joy to work with a director like that."

The Harvey Girls called for a large score, and Warren composed ten songs, two of which were cut after production because of their length. The first song is a gentle, romantic expression by Judy Garland, a Harvey girl from the East, as she contemplates the new and awesome Western landscape:

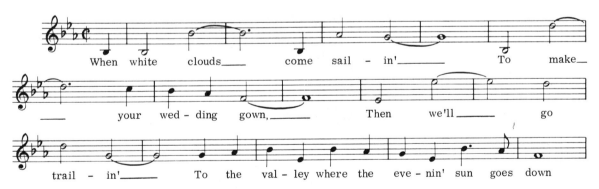

When white clouds___ come sail - in'___ To make___ your wed - ding gown,___ Then we'll___ go trail - in'___ To the val - ley where the eve - nin' sun goes down

Sidney's mobile direction, the Western scenery, George Folsey's photography, and a cast of spirited players make this a film of pleasing entertainment. The songs are a bonus, of which

237

Yolanda and the Thief: Fred Astaire and part of the dream ballet.

Yolanda and the Thief: Lucille
Bremer and Fred Astaire dancing to
the melody of "Will You Marry Me?"

238

"On the Atchison, Topeka and the Santa Fe" is not only a highlight but a milestone in movie musicals. The number runs nine minutes and takes in the entire cast and a vast amount of scenery, growing from the expectation of the train's arrival to a full glorification of its being. Dramatically the jollity makes sense, because the whole Harvey enterprise depended on the railroad.

Once the train has been royally received the Harvey company breaks into "The Train Must Be Fed," as a kind of guide to the waitresses.

That night, Judy and her two waitress friends Cyd Charisse and Virginia O'Brien sing, in their nightgowns, about the joys and sorrows of life as they see it—"It's a Great Big World."

Virginia O'Brien, who specialized in deadpan singing, voices an amusingly wry song about her being something of a plain Jane and her disappointment in the West:

I was hop-in' to be rop-in' some-pin' wild in The Wild, Wild West,___

I been set-tin' till I'm get-tin' kind-a riled at The Wild, Wild West,___

Cyd Charisse, twenty-three years old and making one of her first appearances on the screen, does well for herself in this picture by winning the love of saloon singer and pianist Kenny Baker, for whom Harry Warren found it easy to write a flowing, tenorlike love ballad:

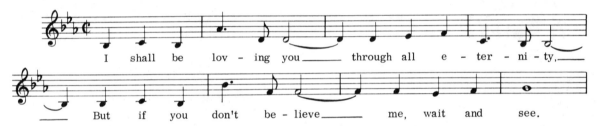

I shall be lov - ing you___ through all e - ter - ni - ty,___

___ But if you don't be - lieve___ me, wait and see.

After he sings the song Charisse glides into a graceful dance expressing her warm response.

This same saloon is also the domain of the lusty Angela Lansbury, an earthy entertainer heading up a team of chorus girls whose deportment and attitude toward the cowboys and railroad workers is considerably different from that of Mr. Harvey's waitresses. This produces a melee between the two sets of females, but not until after Angela has excited male corpuscles with "Oh, You Kid!"

Virtue triumphs in *The Harvey Girls,* and Garland wins the handsome John Hodiak, although their song "My Intuition" was cut from the final print. The final song is the swirling country-dance "Swing Your Partner Round and Round," choreographed by Robert Alton with no-holds-barred gusto.

"On the Atchison, Topeka and the Sante Fe" won an Oscar as the best song of 1946, a third win for Warren. He wrote the melody and fixed the title in its place at the end of the first stanza. Mercer took the lead sheet and, as is his custom, came back several days later with the complete lyrics. Mercer was also at this time one of the founders and leading executives of Capitol Records, and he beat everybody else to the punch by putting out his own recording of the song.

Harry Warren heard the news of his Oscar victory while riding in a car with Harold Arlen, who had won an Oscar for "Over the Rainbow." Neither composer made any comment on hearing the radio announcement, but as they got out of the car Warren said quietly to Arlen, "Walk two Oscars behind me."

The Harvey Girls: "On the Atchison, Topeka and the Santa Fe."

The Harvey Girls: Kenny Baker singing "Wait and See" to Cyd Charisse.

The Harvey Girls: Angela Lansbury knocking the boys dead with "Oh, You Kid."

The Harvey Girls: Virginia O'Brien, Judy Garland and Cyd Charisse singing "It's a Great Big World."

The Harvey Girls: Judy Garland and
the girls dancing "Swing Your
Partner Round and Round."

Harry Warren and lyricist Ralph
Blane working on the score of
"Summer Holiday."

SUMMER HOLIDAY (1948)

Summer Holiday is treasured among connoisseurs of movie musicals and for Harry Warren the favorite of his films. Few movies of its kind received such glowing praise from the critics, and yet the general public was not impressed and the picture made little profit for MGM. Be that as it may, *Summer Holiday* has staunch defenders; critic-commentator Rex Reed places it second on his list of favorite musicals, giving the edge to *Singin' in the Rain*.

The film was shot in the summer of 1946 but not released until May 1948 because Metro was unsure of its market value. This view may seem crass, but the results tend to prove that they knew their business. The market for musicals in the forties was fairly well prescribed, and attempts to do something "different," with a touch of "quality," usually missed the mark. *The Pirate* is another case in point.

Summer Holiday is a musical setting of Eugene O'Neill's play *Ah, Wilderness!* and it succeeds, as did the original, in painting a picture of an America long gone. It is, in fact, a superb piece of Americana. In writing about his portrayal of family life in a small town in 1906, O'Neill said, "Its quality depended upon atmosphere, sentiment, an exact evocation of the mood of a dead past." Producer Arthur Freed and director Rouben Mamoulian followed that opinion to the letter. In hiring Mamoulian, Freed was obviously intent on a quality product. Mamoulian, who always liked to divide his career between the theater and films, had spent the previous five years on Broadway, distinguishing himself as the director of the original productions of *Oklahoma!*, *Carousel*, and *St. Louis Woman*. His concept of *Summer Holiday* could easily lend itself to the theater.

For his lyricist, Warren chose Ralph Blane, who had come to Metro when his *Best Foot Forward*, which he wrote with Hugh Martin, was filmed. Says Warren, "Ralph was the perfect man for this job because he was a collaborator rather than a lyricist who went away and came

Summer Holiday: Mickey Rooney singing "Afraid to Fall in Love" to Gloria De Haven.

back with the words. This was a case where the songs were part of the story, and Ralph deserves more credit than he has received for his work on this picture. Frances Goodrich and Albert Hackett wrote a fine screenplay, but the placement of the songs was mostly Ralph's concept, and he built his lyrics as extensions of the dialogue, very much in the O'Neill mood. It was his idea to open the picture with Walter Huston, as the father–newspaper editor, singing:

Our town is-n't found on the map, tho' we're part of Con-nec-ti-cut.

As Huston finishes his lines about the pleasant little town of Danville, Connecticut, the scene moves to his home, where we meet others of his family—his wife, his sister, Lil, and especially his son, Richard, played by Mickey Rooney—all of whom sing lines of this same song and thereby set their characters. Rooney is about to graduate from high school and he is full of adolescent pretensions. His girlfriend, Gloria De Haven, is reluctant to accept his advances, and he tries to win her over with a sunny and very tuneful ditty:

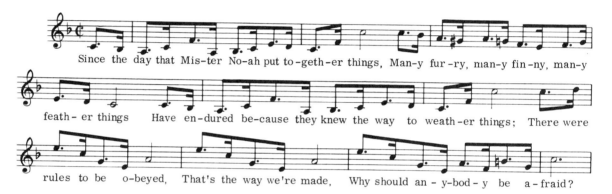

Since the day that Mis-ter No-ah put to-geth-er things, Man-y fur-ry, man-y fin-ny, man-y feath-er things Have en-dured be-cause they knew the way to weath-er things; There were rules to be o-beyed, That's the way we're made, Why should an-y-bod-y be a-fraid?

The song works its spell on Gloria, and she and Mickey then merrily dance over the wide and lovely expanse of green grass in a park.

This sequence was filmed at Busch Gardens in Pasadena and delightfully photographed in Technicolor by Charles Schoenbaum. All the photography in *Summer Holiday* is of an exceptionally high and artistic standard.

The graduation ceremonies are loud and spirited, with students singing and marching to the song "All Hail to Danville High," followed by Rooney's comically pompous valedictory. This leads to a ride in the family car and the hit song of *Summer Holiday*, "The Stanley Steamer," a cheery, bouncing song involving most of the family.

The mood has little time to relax as the town launches into its celebration of the Fourth of July:

It's In-de-pen-dence Day Down the hatch and roll the kegs a-way;—

The Independence Day sequence is extensive and includes street scenes, a band in the park, picnics, dancing, a beer-drinking contest, romancing, and much singing.

At the end of the day Rooney goes downtown in pursuit of further pleasure and meets a sultry, sexy cabaret singer, Marilyn Maxwell, who chants "The Weary Blues" and tantalizes Rooney. Engaged in which he thinks is his first adult adventure, Rooney drinks more and more, with Marilyn becoming ever more erotic in his eyes. She sings to him, "I Think You're the

246

Summer Holiday: The picnic dance.

Summer Holiday: At the Fourth of July picnic, and to the strains of "Independence Day," Walter Huston taunts Frank Morgan with a glass of beer.

Summer Holiday: Mickey Rooney,
Gloria De Haven, Agnes Moorehead,
Walter Huston, Selena Royle and
Butch Jenkins in "The Stanley
Steamer."

On the set of *Summer Holiday*,
Marilyn Maxwell rehearses "I Think
You're the Sweetest Kid I've Ever
Known" with Mickey Rooney.

248

Sweetest Kid I've Ever Known," but by this time Rooney is too intoxicated to do anything but stagger home. This sequence originally included a fantasy in which Rooney imagines himself as Omar Khayyam in love with a princess—told in song—but it was cut, much to the regret of Rooney, Warren, and Blane.

The young hero recovers from his hangover; he has a heart-to-heart talk with his father and tells him he has decided to settle down with his girlfriend and live a good, solid life. The picture ends on a note of domestic concord and a reprise of "Afraid to Fall in Love."

This was not the ending as originally written. Throughout the picture Rooney has been quoting great poets including a lot of Omar Khayyam. At the end, as originally scripted, Huston and his wife gaze fondly at Mickey and Gloria as they walk away hand in hand, and Huston takes a pointer from his son and quotes Khayyam: "Ah, that spring should vanish with the rose." Then he sighs and says, "Well, spring isn't everything, is it, Essie?"

The script then called for Huston and his wife to sing "Spring Isn't Everything," but it was decided to cut this. Also cut was a song in which Frank Morgan, as amiable, tippling Uncle Sid, courts Cousin Lil, Agnes Moorehead, and promises to change his ways if she will marry him. The cuts were brutal, in the opinion of those who worked on the picture, and a blind attempt on the part of MGM to bring the picture down to what they considered a more marketable ninety minutes. Particularly regrettable to Harry Warren was the cutting of "Spring Isn't Everything," which he considers to be among his best songs:

Warren's contract with MGM called for his retaining ownership of any material cut from a picture. He later published this song—and others—for his own company, Four Jays Music Inc., but it was small compensation for the loss of its proper place in the context of *Summer Holiday*.

Summer Holiday: Ralph Blane and Harry Warren present a copy of their score to director Rouben Mamoulian.

249

"None of us quite understood why the picture didn't fare better with the public," Warren says. "Perhaps the timing was wrong, and perhaps it had best been done on the stage. Blane and I thought of doing that but then somebody came up with another musical based on the O'Neill play—*Take Me Along*. However, it's good to know the film has so many admirers. I loved doing it—it was just the kind of picture I'd hoped for, one in which I could be involved with the planning and the production the way a composer is in the theater. In thirty years of writing songs for pictures I rarely had projects that really interested me. This one did. But the money, of course, always came with the more conventional pictures."

THE BARKLEYS OF BROADWAY (1949)

The Barkleys of Broadway was designed as a follow-up for Fred Astaire and Judy Garland after their great success with *Easter Parade*, but Garland was taken off the project because of ill health just as it was about to go into production. By this time she had developed the neurotic, uneven temperament that would soon cause her career to collapse. Ginger Rogers was quickly brought in, uniting her with Astaire after a screen separation of ten years. The fans had long been clamoring for another Astaire-Rogers picture, which made the lack of Garland less of a loss than it might have been.

Despite his desire to do the lyrics, producer Arthur Freed suggested to Harry Warren that they bring in someone else. Warren says, "It happened that Ira Gershwin's agent had asked me to put the word around that Ira was interested in working. Everyone always assumes that famous people don't need work. I mentioned this to Freed, and after the usual negotiations Ira signed a contract. He and Arthur had long known each other, but in working together on this picture they became close friends. From then on Arthur became one of the elite at the Gershwin dinner table, which usually seated the intelligentsia of the theater crowd.

"This was fine except that it had a little backlash for me. Freed became so much a part of the Gershwin clan that he decided he had to have a great Gershwin song in *The Barkleys*. He picked 'They Can't Take That Away From Me.' I didn't take kindly to this—not that I didn't like the song, but there isn't a composer alive who likes having a song by someone else interpolated into his score."

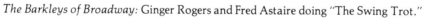

The Barkleys of Broadway: Ginger Rogers and Fred Astaire doing "The Swing Trot."

The Barkleys of Broadway: Fred Astaire and all those "Shoes With Wings On."

The screenplay by Betty Comden and Adolph Green is light and witty but fairly conventional in plot. Astaire and Rogers are a married couple, famed as musical-comedy stars on Broadway, who bicker incessantly. The picture opens joyously as they dance on stage to Warren's bouncy "Swing Trot." Later, in the dressing room, it becomes necessary for Fred to soothe the frazzled Ginger and reassure her of his love:

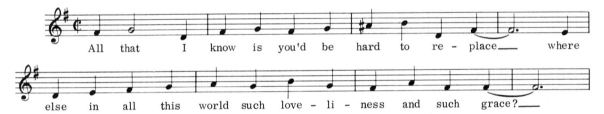

All that I know is you'd be hard to re - place___ where else in all this world such love - li - ness and such grace?___

Another Warren instrumental number, "Bouncin' the Blues," is heard in a rehearsal sequence, and afterward the couple does a routine on stage in kilts and Scottish tweeds, slightly hampered by thick accents as they sing a song of greatly restrained passion:

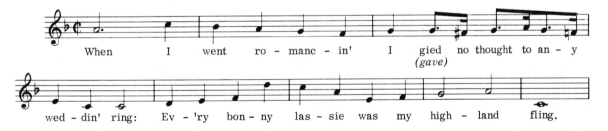

When I went ro - manc - in' I gied (*gave*) no thought to an - y wed - din' ring: Ev - 'ry bon - ny las - sie was my high - land fling.

The conflict in *The Barkleys of Broadway* comes when Ginger gets delusions of grandeur about being a dramatic actress and decides to split up with her husband when he refuses to take her seriously. Complicating the matter is a handsome French director, Jacques Francois, who encourages Ginger to become the tragedienne of her desire and at the same time hopes to win her heart.

Fortunately Oscar Levant is around most of the time as the sardonic friend of Fred and

251

The Barkleys of Broadway: Ginger Rogers and Fred Astaire doing "My One and Only Highland Fling."

The Barkleys of Broadway:

Ginger, and his quips help lighten this rather mundane situation. At one glorious point in the picture the reluctant Levant joins the pair as they take a brisk walk down a country lane during a weekend at the home of mutual friends. Sadly, when MGM issued the sound-track recording of this score they decided to drop "A Weekend in the Country," thereby denying song collectors a comic gem:

A week-end in the coun-try__ nev-er will let you down.__ You'll par-don my ef-front-'ry,__ I'd rath-er spend it in town.__ A week-end in the coun-try__ keep-ing your health at par,__ As on the grass-y green we fro-lic, 'Mid the fields of rye we rol-lick, Give me rye that's al-co-hol-ic frol-ic-ing at a bar!

Ginger succeeds in her ambition to become a dramatic actress, although her scene as Sarah Bernhardt reciting "La Marseillaise" is hard to take. What she doesn't realize is that it's her devoted husband who keeps coming on the telephone with a French accent giving her instructions on how to act her role. Eventually the truth dawns on her, and even though she's proved her ability with drama she elects to return to the musical stage—and her husband.

To bring the picture to a close, Fred and Ginger dance "The Manhattan Downbeat," he in his familiar top hat, white tie, and tales and she in a flowing gown. How else should a "together again" movie with Astaire and Rogers end?

In addition to the musical numbers already mentioned, *The Barkleys of Broadway* contains two other dances. One is a duet at a benefit show in which the estranged pair get together for the sake of charity to do "They Can't Take That Away from Me." The other, "Shoes with Wings On," is an Astaire solo and a high point in his catalog of distinctive, imaginative dances. The Warren melody has a solid beat at the end of every second bar and was obviously written to be danced to. Astaire choreographed it with the help of Hermes Pan, who worked with the dancer on many of his creations.

Barkleys is filled with dancing expertise; it was directed by Charles Walters, who had only recently switched from choreography to direction, and the remainder of the dances were designed by Robert Alton. Once again the musical direction of Lennie Hayton and the arrangements of Conrad Salinger ring loud and clear in their skill.

"Shoes with Wings On" is a show within the show; Astaire is a cobbler who tries on a pair of dancing shoes and finds them magical. Then, as the Sorcerer's Apprentice, things get out of control, with dozens of pairs of shoes becoming wildly animated and Fred resorting to battle to quell them. The jaunty song is so typically Astaire in its blithe phrasing that it could only have been tailor-made for him.

Harry Warren worked with Astaire on four productions and looks back on the association with pleasure. "This is the gentleman's gentleman," Warren says, "and unlike anybody else in the business. He's the most retiring, most polite, and quietest man I've worked with. We had discussions on his dances, on ideas for them. He would tell me what he had in mind, and I

would play melodies for him. If he liked them I would write them down, and he would take them away. Sometimes he would come back a few days later and almost apologetically explain that he had tried a piece out and couldn't get it to work. Could I write something else? With Fred it was a pleasure."

MY DREAM IS YOURS (1949)

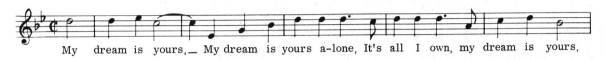

My dream is yours,_ My dream is yours a-lone, It's all I own, my dream is yours,

Harry Warren returned to Warners late in 1948 at the request of Leo Forbstein, who was still the head of the music department. It was among the last things Forbstein did before his sudden death of a heart attack. Ray Heindorf took over the position and also acted as music director on *My Dream Is Yours*. In that respect it was like coming home for Warren. "But it had been almost ten years since I worked there," he says, "and much had changed. It was a little like going back to a town you once lived in as a youngster. The streets seem narrower and the buildings smaller. The atmosphere had changed a lot—it seemed less frenetic, and it was a little strange to work with people I hadn't seen in years. Except for Jack Warner, the executives were a different lot, although the imperious way they treated talent seemed about the same. I remember after Ralph Blane and I—I'd taken him with me from Metro—played the songs for the brass, one of the executives, Alex Gottlieb, asked 'You have only six hits in this picture?' I replied, 'Six hits? I'll settle for one!' "

My Dream Is Yours was Doris Day's second film, made as a follow-up to her popular *Romance on the High Seas*. Both were directed by Warners' mighty workhorse Michael Curtiz, who seemingly could make a success of any kind of picture. Says Warren, "Mike had a reputation for being tough with actors, but I think he had a soft spot for songwriters. He was a mad Hungarian with a ferocious accent, and if he liked a song I had just played him he would embrace me." Such conviviality perhaps concealed from Warren the realization that what he was working on was a limp backstage musical, set in radio and not much better than the plots used in the Warner musicals of the early thirties.

Doris Day appears in this one as a singer hoping for The Big Break. Along comes a snappy advertising man—Jack Carson in a part that would undoubtedly have gone to Pat O'Brien in previous times—and he picks her up when his main claim to income, crooner Lee Bowman, walks out on him at the termination of his contract. Carson persuades Doris to make the trip to Hollywood, where he manages to get her the radio spot vacated by Bowman. To the dismay of Carson, who loves her, she falls for the heel crooner. But eventually she realizes the caliber of both men and makes the right choice.

The picture is overlong for its material, running a hefty hundred minutes, and sadly lacks a little Berkeley production magic to lift it. The burden of the singing falls on Doris Day, with a little help from Carson, an actor who could handle almost any kind of material and yet never received any great credit. The most sparkling sequence of this film is a Bugs Bunny animation with the two stars, using the song "Freddie, Get Ready." Another highlight is Doris and pop pianist Frankie Carle performing "Canadian Capers," with new lyrics by both Warren and Blane.

"Love Finds a Way" never found its way into the hearts of the public despite a pretty melody, and the novelty song "Tick, Tick, Tick" deftly compared the love-stricken heart to the atomic bomb.

The Barkleys of Broadway: Ginger and Fred and the "Manhattan Downbeat."

My Dream is Yours: Doris Day doing the title song.

My Dream is Yours: Lee Bowman, as the conceited crooner, with Ada Leonard leading the all-girl group in "Love Finds a Way."

My Dream is Yours: Doris Day and Ada Leonard wait for the announcer's cue.

Pagan Love Song: Howard Keel and
Esther Williams.

Aside from the new songs, a good many old Warren and Dubin numbers were used, including a memorable and sultry rendition of "I'll String Along with You" by Doris. According to Warren, "She was very easy to work with. Years of singing with bands had given her the poise and the confidence, plus musical savvy, that made a transition to the movies relatively easy for her. She was friendly, yet there was a remoteness about her that is typical of so many stars. Maybe that's their way of protecting themselves, but it's as if they lived on the other side of the river." Be that as it may, Harry Warren was grateful that Doris Day recorded and popularized the title song from *My Dream Is Yours* and "Someone Like You," giving him two more hits.

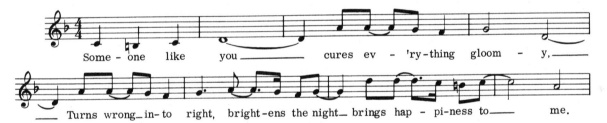

PAGAN LOVE SONG (1950)

Pagan Love Song was originally titled *Tahiti*, with Harry Warren and Arthur Freed writing a suitably rhapsodic title song for lusty baritone-hero Howard Keel:

But with the film almost completed, Freed had a change of mind and decided to use a song he and Nacio Herb Brown had written in 1929 for Ramon Novarro to sing in *The Pagan.* Says Warren, "We had some nasty words about this, but Arthur not only had the vanity that is common to all songwriters, but he was the boss, so I was on the losing end of the argument. Unfortunately, this followed a similar situation on *The Barkleys of Broadway,* and once again I felt myself falling out of love with a studio.

"I think another reason Freed used his old song was that he was just too busy to come up with any more new lyrics. My feeling was that he shouldn't have done the lyrics for this picture at all. He was too busy, but he was torn between his love of writing songs and his tremendous schedule as a producer. Right before this one he had produced *On the Town* and *Annie Get Your Gun*, and he followed it with *Royal Wedding*, *Show Boat*, and *An American in Paris*. All this in the space of two years, and all of it good. An incredible output."

Pagan Love Song is the least of the Freed musicals of this period. Metro had the problem of finding suitable properties for the popular aquatic star Esther Williams, and at this time they also needed a vehicle for Howard Keel to follow up his successful screen debut in *Annie Get Your Gun*. A story about an American in a tropical paradise seemed logical. Here Keel is a schoolteacher from Ohio who arrives in Tahiti to take over the coconut plantation of his late uncle and readily takes to the happy-go-lucky atmosphere. Even the bamboo house in which he lives causes him to break into song:

It takes Keel no time at all to discover that the most beautiful girl on the island is Esther Williams. She, of course, is only part Polynesian, and American by birth. Soon she and Keel are merrily traipsing around the island and following the local custom of "Singing in the Sun," thanks to Warren and Freed. In private she practices her swimming and croons a lovely song in her contentment:

The plot of *Pagan Love Song* moves all the way from A to B and back again. Keel informally adopts a group of local youngsters and announces his plan to marry Esther. But they have a falling-out when Keel's young helpers ignore his crop in favor of the celebrations on Bastille Day, with Esther taking their side. Keel prepares to leave Tahiti in disgust, but the youngsters save his crop and bring the lovers back together. "Why Is Love So Crazy?" neatly sums up Keel's happy wonderment:

The Warren melodies for *Pagan Love Song* are pleasant, but none of them attained the exalted rank of standards. All the songs were released as commercial recordings, as soundtrack material, which by 1950 had become popular with the record-buying public. Most of the film was shot at the studio but Hawaiian location shots were interspliced, and Tahitian dancers were brought in. Robert Alton, who had made his name as a choreographer, directed the picture, and his touch is most apparent in the Williams water ballets. And despite the common practice of dubbing stars with limited voices, it is indeed Esther singing the lovely, seductive "The Sea of the Moon."

Pagan Love Song: Esther Williams and Howard Keel, and "The House of Singing Bamboo."

Howard Keel, lyricist-producer Arthur Freed and Harry Warren, during the recording session for *Pagan Love Song*.

SUMMER STOCK (1950)

Summer Stock, produced by Joe Pasternak (Arthur Freed did not produce *every* Metro musical, although it seems a pity he didn't), had some fine ingredients in Judy Garland, Gene Kelly, and a half dozen songs by Harry Warren, reunited with Mack Gordon. However, its hokey show-biz story is a step-down from the quality Metro had achieved with films like *On the Town*, *Summer Holiday*, and *The Pirate*. This might have been a film Garland and Rooney would have done in 1940. It was also a painful picture to make because of Garland's sicknesses and her unreliable behavior, resulting in its being her last work for MGM.

Summer Stock was in production for eight months, twice the time originally planned. Garland spent three months of convalescence in a Boston clinic before production and returned to the studio plumper than she had ever been. Years of nervous strain had affected her sense of security, and there were many days on which she could not appear before the cameras. However, very little of her traumatized condition is apparent in this film, which opens on a bright and breezy note with Judy in the shower, singing the kind of song most people would like to be able to sing in the shower:

If you feel like sing - ing, sing,_____ Tra - la - la your cares a - way

For its British release the title of the film was changed to *If You Feel Like Singing*, since the American theatrical term *summer stock* has no such meaning in the British Isles. In the film Judy portrays a young lady farmer, running her property against odds. She has a stagestruck younger sister, Gloria de Haven, who brings a theatrical troupe led by Gene Kelly to the farm to stage their musical because they have nowhere else to do it. Judy resists, but relents in return for their promise to help with the chores. This they do, with some obvious comic mishaps, and Kelly cajoles Judy into becoming a performer herself.

Just before the young band of thespians arrives, Judy is seen driving her new tractor from town to her farm, feeling full of accomplishment and goodwill toward her fellow toilers of the soil, singing:

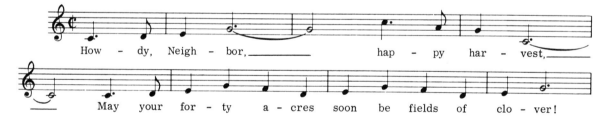

How - dy, Neigh - bor,_____ hap - py har - vest,___

_____ May your for - ty a - cres soon be fields of clo - ver!

After Kelly and his company agree to supply services in return for their keep, he and his sidekick, Phil Silvers, sing the jivey "Dig, Dig, Dig, Dig for Your Supper." The following morning Kelly sets up shop in the barn and starts rehearsals. He directs Gloria and her leading man, Hans Conreid, in a hammy spoof of summer-stock heroes, in their love ballad, "Memory Island," which itself is a spoof of old-fashioned theater ballads:

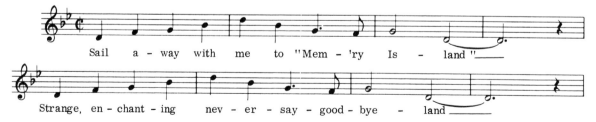

Sail a - way with me to "Mem - 'ry Is - land "_____

Strange, en - chant - ing nev - er - say - good - bye - land___

Summer Stock: Gene Kelly dancing to "Dig, Dig, Dig, Dig for Your Dinner."

Summer Stock: Judy Garland singing "Howdy Neighbor, Happy Harvest."

261

Summer Stock: Gene Kelly showing Gloria De Haven and Hans Conried how he wants "Memory Island" delivered.

As a solo for Judy, Warren and Gordon wrote a gentle song to express her loneliness and her desire for love. She sings it by herself at night, gazing into the starry skies:

Friend - ly   star,   where can you be hid-ing   Smile for me from out of the lone -ly night

Kelly overhears her singing and also catches her by herself trying a few dance steps on stage. He senses that she has a taste for the theater, which he encourages while falling in love with her. He expresses this love in "You, Wonderful You," a simple little song that caught the public fancy. Later in the picture it is also used by Kelly as a solo dance, as he wanders around the deserted stage at night, uncertain of the outcome of his show or his relationship with Judy. Here Kelly artfully uses the squeaking boards of the stage and a spread page of newspaper to build up his dance.

I'm   glad   I   met   you,   you   won- der - ful   you,_____
_____   I   won't   for - get   you,_____   you   won- der - ful   you.

Harry Warren was not happy working on *Summer Stock*. He had been given his choice of lyricist and asked for Mack Gordon, who had been dropped by Fox and, like most of the song-writers in Hollywood, was looking for work. Warren feels that Gordon was treated with little respect at MGM. The musical unit of that studio was tight, flushed with success and clearly overflowing with conspicuous talent. Gordon had failed in his attempts to become a producer at Fox, and he had alienated many people with his brusque, commanding manner. At Metro, he suffered a blow to his pride when his lyrics for "You, Wonderful You" were dumped and a new set were supplied by Jack Brooks and Saul Chaplin. Warren was off the picture by this time and had no say in the matter. It proved to be one of the last films on which Mack Gordon worked. He died in March 1959 at the age of fifty-five, and Warren feels his death was partly the result of his cutting his great weight by a hundred pounds. Like Al Dubin, Gordon was a man of girth and appetite, and also like Dubin, he died early because of it.

Two new songs, "Heavenly Music" and "All for You," were added to *Summer Stock* after Warren had finished his commitment. These were by other songwriters, which annoyed Warren, but not as much as the addition of "Get Happy" two months after the rest of the film had been completed. Warren considers these additions as desperate attempts on the part of Gene Kelly and director Charles Walters to improve the picture.

Warren says, "It was a sad experience working with Judy at this time. She had always been a little strange—one day she would greet you warmly and the next ignore you—but she was ill a lot of the time on this picture. When we came to record 'You, Wonderful You,' her voice was heavy and dull, and we couldn't use it. Months later, after she had another spell of convalescence, she came back and recorded 'Get Happy' and sounded terrific. She was also twenty pounds lighter, which is why this sequence looks as if it's been spliced in from another picture.

"Everybody came away from the movie talking about how great she was doing 'Get Happy,' which was tough for me to swallow, since I had been hired to write the score. They didn't consult me, and Harold Arlen and Ted Koehler, who wrote the song, had no say either. They were happy about it, of course, but songwriters are touchy people.

"The Garland fans liked it too, but even with that, Metro let her go. They were tightening their belts, and she was just too much trouble and too costly. However, I think she was treated

Summer Stock: Judy Garland and
Gene Kelly singing "You, Wonderful
You."

265

better at MGM than at any other studio. If she'd been at Warners they would have dropped her years before. Louis B. Mayer was quite paternal with her, despite all the unkind things they say about him, and he kept her on as long as he could."

TEXAS CARNIVAL (1951)

Of his MGM musicals, Harry Warren considers *Texas Carnival* the poorest of them. Again the director was Charles Walters, but the producer was Jack Cummings, who, along with Joe Pasternak, vied with Arthur Freed in making the studio's musicals. Cummings stood little chance of matching the Freed record with this one. Warren and the late lyricist Dorothy Fields wrote a large amount of material for the film but only four of their songs were used. The running time of seventy-six minutes suggests a certain amount of cutting.

The plot deals with Red Skelton and Esther Williams as carnival-show performers. He is the pitchman—and delivers a rousing song, "The Carnie's Pitch"—and she is a swimmer who takes dunks when the customers succeed in hitting her cage with balls.

An alcoholic Texas millionaire, Keenan Wynn, takes a shine to Skelton and invites him to his swank hotel, where Red is mistaken for the millionaire. With Wynn absent, Red lives the life of a Texas Reilly, with Esther assumed to be his sister.

The foreman of the Wynn ranch is Howard Keel, who is torn between his fascination for Esther and his concern for his boss. The concern is merely a delaying factor in the picture, marking time before the inevitable love affair. Keel sings the film's two ballads, one of which is in the best baritone cowboy tradition, sung to a horse:

Whoa, Em - ma! Be - have your - self___ Whoa, Em - ma! My
sil - ly lit - tle fil - ly, take it slow! Em - ma and save your - self!___

Texas Carnival: Red Skelton doing the carnie pitch. The girl in the gilded cage is Esther Williams.

Texas Carnival: Howard Keel and Esther Williams.

Texas Carnival includes an Esther Williams aqua ballet, this one a dream sequence in which she seemingly swims around Keel's room to vamp him. More interesting, at least musically, is the appearance of Ann Miller as the girl who wins Skelton's heart, when she sings and dances "It's Dynamite." This is staged at a party for the wealthy Texans. The picture ends with Skelton coming in first in a chuck-wagon race and winning enough money to pay off his poker debts.

On the credit side, the film does manage some good-natured ribbing of Texas but any mention of the film causes Harry Warren to shake his head. "I didn't like it," he says, "and it was an unhappy experience. This was the only time I worked with a lady lyricist—and she was the best—but we didn't have that rapport songwriting needs. She was a rather aggressive woman, and I'm kind of turned off by aggression. Dorothy would call me at all hours, even seven in the morning, to discuss lyrics, but what rankled most was her telling me I was wasting my time in Hollywood, and why didn't I go back and write for the New York theater? That was a thought I'd been trying to put behind me for years."

The best song in *Texas Carnival* is one in favor of marriage that Howard Keel sings in courting Esther Williams. The lyrics were somewhat slight for Keel's impressive voice, but the melody is persuasive:

Texas Carnival: Ann Miller singing and dancing "It's Dynamite."

THE BELLE OF NEW YORK (1952)

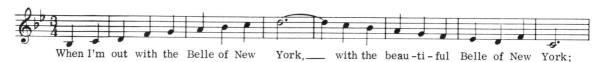

When I'm out with the Belle of New York,___ with the beau-ti-ful Belle of New York;

In its original form *The Belle of New York* was one of the first American operettas, with book and lyrics by Hugh Morton and music by German-born Gustave Kerker. It was first staged in New York in 1897 and survived as a stock piece for many years. It had been a favorite of Arthur Freed's since his days as a stagestruck youngster, and he first discussed the idea of making it into a film with Fred Astaire while they were making *Yolanda and the Thief.*

Astaire declined, feeling that it was a thin and far too old-fashioned vehicle for the screen. It was a bad time to present any vehicle to Astaire because he wanted to retire—and did, until two years of inactivity drove him to resume his career.

The persistent Freed faced Astaire with the project again in 1951, and this time the dancer agreed to do the film provided the book was rewritten and given a completely new score.

268

The idea of giving it to Harry Warren and Johnny Mercer met with his immediate approval. It might be argued that Astaire should have stuck with his original stand not to make this film. This is far from his best work on the screen, and yet with nine songs spaced over an unusually brief eighty-two minutes, *The Belle of New York* is at least a pleasing divertissement.

The film's basic problem is lack of story and an implausible leading man. Here Astaire is a charming, irresponsible Lothario dependent on a prudish Victorian aunt, Marjorie Main, for his income. So far he has left five brides-to-be waiting at the church in vain. Then he discovers Vera-Ellen, a social worker employed at a mission sponsored by his aunt, and falls in love with her. Other men have done the same, and in unison they sing the title song under her window, not that any of them have actually been out with this straitlaced, dedicated young lady. Astaire expresses his joy in loving her by dancing through the streets and engaging in various gravity-defying stunts, thanks to MGM's special effects.

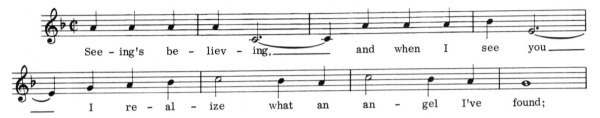

Up to this point the lovable rake has been frequenting an elegant house of ill repute. Now he gives the girls a farewell party and sings about his change of plans, "The Bachelor's Dinner Song," in which he asks, "Who wants to kiss the bridegroom, on his last night out?"

Despite his optimism, Astaire finds courting Vera-Ellen difficult. But he promises to become a solid citizen, and as proof he gets a job as a streetcar conductor. This pleases her, and she responds agreeably when he sings "Baby Doll":

The Belle of New York: Fred Astaire, with friends, doing "The Bachelor's Dinner Song."

The Belle of New York: The Currier and Ives sequence.

The Belle of New York: Fred Astaire, trying to persuade Vera-Ellen that she's his "Baby Doll."

270

The song became the only hit from this score. Vera-Ellen's singing of this and the other songs was dubbed by Anita Ellis.

While on duty with his streetcar Astaire takes time off to dance and sing with Vera-Ellen a song that expresses his lighthearted reaction to winning her:

Vera-Ellen's own reaction to getting married is far more romantic and fanciful. She sings "The Bride's Wedding Song" and imagines herself dancing with Astaire through the four seasons in settings inspired by Currier and Ives prints. Artistically this is the highlight of the film and further evidence of the skill of art directors Cedric Gibbons and Jack Martin Smith, both of whom worked with distinction during this period of MGM history.

Despite the power of love, however, Astaire gets drunk the night before his wedding and sleeps through much of the following day. Convinced that he really isn't good enough for Vera-Ellen, he breaks off the engagement. She takes a different view and in an attempt to get him back she assumes the guise of a sexy vamp, and dressed in a lacy black dress she sets out to tantalize him:

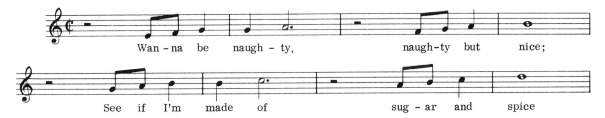

The Belle of New York: Vera-Ellen and Fred Astaire dancing in the clouds to the tune of "Seeing's Believing."

Astaire is more impressed with her persistence than with her vamping, and he jumps to her defense when a masher makes the kind of advances vamping usually provokes. The scene, a nightclub, is turned into a shambles in the ensuing brawl, but it succeeds in bringing the lovers together.

With that achieved, the film gets on with the real business—letting Fred Astaire dance, which he does with great gusto in a song that states simply enough, "I Wanna Be a Dancin' Man." Dressed in a white suit and with no props except a sand-sprinkled floor, Fred nimbly taps and shuffles his claim to fame:

The Belle of New York required a great deal of cinematic wizardry to achieve such effects as Astaire and Vera-Ellen dancing in the clouds and various tricks in the production numbers, and it took more time than Freed had expected. Says Warren, "I liked the picture even though it was old-fashioned, and it called for a big score, which I also liked. But what Mercer and I liked most was getting twenty-four weeks of work out of it. They kept saying they were having troubles making it, and we kept hoping they would find more and more problems."

SKIRTS AHOY! (1952)

The Belle of New York was Harry Warren's last film with Arthur Freed's highly esteemed unit. It wasn't as such—it simply happened that way. By the same token, when Warren accepted Joe Pasternak's invitation to score Skirts Ahoy! he did not realize that it would be his final work at MGM. The pity is that his last Metro musical could not have been a sturdier vehicle.

Skirts Ahoy! which glorifies the distaff life in the navy, is pleasing and amusing but lacks any real impact. Warren again called for Ralph Blane—who always had to fly in from his rural home in Broken Arrow, Oklahoma—and they wrote seven numbers, including the obligatory marching song for the titles. Warren, ever the lover of band music, built his melody along the lines of bugle calls, and music director Georgie Stoll and orchestrator Pete Rugolo took advantage of this with hefty brass and percussion sections.

As expected, the picture, filmed partly at the Great Lakes Naval Training Depot, includes a good amount of drill and parade performance. It also, surprisingly, includes a formal-dance sequence with a graceful melody in three-quarter time:

Dressed in na - vy blue_____ we danced The Na - vy Waltz___

___ Till the night was through___ we danced The Na - vy Waltz

Skirts Ahoy! has Esther Williams, Vivian Blaine, and Joan Evans as a trio who join the navy either to get away from male problems or to find them. Esther is the elegant one, a rich girl running away from an unhappy marriage; Vivian is eager to marry but has trouble pinning down her sailor boyfriend, so she joins up to be near him; and Joan puts on the uniform because she has been left standing at the altar.

The script serves merely to link the songs, two swimming sequences by Esther, and sundry romantic complications. After the picture was in production, producer Pasternak, probably sensing that he needed a little extra boost, arranged for Debbie Reynolds and Bobby Van to do a guest appearance as themselves at a naval show, singing and dancing to an old vaudeville number, "Oh, by Jingo." Again Warren was not consulted about an interpolation into his score, and much as he objected, he had come to accept it as a fact of Metro life. As he puts it, "The only way you could be autonomous at a studio in those days was if they really needed

Skirts Ahoy!: Esther Williams leading the Waves at the Great Lakes Naval Training Station, to the beat of the title song.

you, the way they needed people like Astaire and Kelly. They could dictate terms. Anyone less was considered a hireling. If they paid you well they figured they owned you."

Billy Eckstine also makes a guest appearance in *Skirts Ahoy!* singing the sultry "Hold Me Close to You," a moderately successful song for a short while. The five De Marco Sisters are also on hand throughout the picture, helping with the musical chores. They assist Esther in the slightly slapstick comedy song "What Makes a Wave?" and the rousing "Glad to Have You Aboard." Perhaps the most appealing melody in the score is:

As with all service musicals, the action is fairly well prescribed. In fact, *Skirts Ahoy!* might well have been called *Shipmates Forever Revisited*. Esther ends up with naval doctor Barry Sullivan, Vivian keeps hoping to land her sailor, and the timid Joan finds romance in the arms of Keefe Brasselle. And as a recruiting poster for the WAVES, the picture does no harm at all, other than possibly making the service appear a little more exciting than it really is. However, without its eight musical sequences *Skirts Ahoy!* would be a very limp piece of celluloid. The most memorable song is the salty "What Good Is a Gal without a Guy?" put across with complete conviction by Esther, Vivian, and Joan:

With *Skirts Ahoy!* completed, Harry Warren discussed various tentative projects but nothing came into being and by mutual agreement he terminated his contract with MGM. Once again a cycle had played itself out, with Warren coming in on its crest and going out with its ebb.

Unfortunately, there would be no new cycle for the Hollywood musical. Television had made itself felt in 1949, and the film industry soon realized that the new medium would drain its market and its talent. It also quickly became apparent that the first major casualty of the new era was the movie musical. Television variety shows presented song-and-dance productions in copious quantities, almost always using old songs, and at the same time old movie musicals cropped up in video in great numbers, giving Hollywood the severe problem of competing with its own past.

Metro's high points in musicals were *Singin' in the Rain* in 1952 and *The Bandwagon* the following year. After that the mighty Metro music department reduced its ranks. Within a year, a star of the magnitude of Gene Kelly went from great popularity to doubts about the future of his career, while Fred Astaire comforted himself with the knowledge that he had wanted to retire anyway. Arthur Freed produced an average of one picture a year for the remainder of the fifties and retired in 1960. Occasional musicals were made after 1953, but in most cases they were film versions of Broadway shows.

Skirts Ahoy!: Esther Williams and fellow inmates performing chores and singing "What Makes a Wave?"

Skirts Ahoy!: Joan Evans, Esther Williams and Vivian Blaine singing "What Good is a Gal Without a Guy?"

Says Warren, "It was as if the songwriting trade had suddenly ceased to be in demand. It wasn't too bad for me, because I still had offers over the next few years to write songs for pictures, but a lot of the writers were out of work. If it hadn't been for royalties from old songs they would have been in trouble. It seemed to me a tragedy that the Metro musicals had to come to an end, because they were good bits of entertainment, and they employed the best people in the business. It was a marvelous community of musicians, arrangers, composers, conductors, singers, and coaches. A great atmosphere.

"I had had my fights with Freed, but by and large he was a fine man to work for, and Louis B. Mayer was the best boss I ever had. I threatened to quit in 1950 because I didn't like the way Metro's music publishers were handling my songs—I thought they weren't promoting as well as they should and getting enough play on the material. As soon as Mayer heard that, he called me to his office and wanted to know what was wrong. After I told him he said he would remedy it right away and set me up with my own music-publishing company, with an office on Broadway.

"It turned out that the same people would run Harry Warren Music Inc. as ran all the other Metro subsidiaries, so it really didn't make much difference. But it was good for my ego and a good gesture from Mayer. I liked him, and I liked my years at Metro. I'm glad I was a part of it."

This Heart of Mine

Lyric by
ARTHUR FREED
a.s.c.a.p.

Music by
HARRY WARREN
a.s.c.a.p.

On the Atchison, Topeka and the Santa Fe

Lyric by
JOHNNY MERCER

Music by
HARRY WARREN

The Stanley Steamer

Lyric by
RALPH BLANE

Music by
HARRY WARREN

Shoes With Wings On

Lyric by
IRA GERSHWIN

Music by
HARRY WARREN

Refrain, Moderately with a good beat

When I've got Shoes With Wings On ___ The win-ter's gone, the spring's on ___ When

I've got Shoes With Wings On ___ The town is full of rhy-thm and the world's in rhyme. The

Ne-on Cit-y glows up ___ My pret-ty, pret-ty shows up ___ We'll dance un-til they close ___

___ up. ___ Got my guard-i-an an-gel work-ing o-ver-time. ___ I give a-

lad-din the lamp, ___ Mi-das the gold, Who needs a wiz-ard or ma-

PART FIVE

PARAMOUNT
AND TWILIGHT

Spring is here and all the pret-ty flow'rs that grow, grow just for you.

Harry Warren's association with Paramount came about through a phone call from Bing Crosby. "He called at six o'clock one morning," Warren recalls. "It was the first time I'd ever heard from him, and I thought at first it might be someone's practical joke, but as I collected my wits from being woken up I realized it was actually Bing. He asked if I was working, and I said I wasn't. He then asked if I'd like to do a score for him, and I told him I'd be happy to."

Crosby wanted to know who Warren would like as his lyricist. Johnny Mercer's name was mentioned, but Mercer wasn't available and Crosby suggested Leo Robin. This met with Warren's approval—they had worked well together on *The Gang's All Here*—and the deal was set. The choice of Robin was an easy one for Crosby, since he had introduced a good many of the songs Robin had written for Paramount musicals with Ralph Rainger.

Just for You called for the biggest score Warren had written in years, with a total of eleven songs, of which one was cut after production because they felt its purpose was redundant. This first exposure to working for Bing Crosby turned out to be one of the smoothest associations of Warren's career. He says, "We played all the songs for Crosby over a couple of days and in each case it was a polite nod of approval, with a 'fine' at the end. No fuss, no bother. The only time we saw him was when he was on the set when he was working, and there were no problems."

The film needed so many songs because Bing here appears as a songwriting Broadway producer. Robert Carson's screenplay is based on the story "Famous," by Stephen Vincent Benét, and directed by Elliott Nugent. Crosby and his leading lady, Jane Wyman, had appeared together with great success the previous year in *Here Comes the Groom*, and this picture was made to team them again.

293

Mr. and Mrs. Harry Warren at home.

This time Wyman portrays a musical-comedy star who is loved by her producer, a widower. He is about to propose, when his teenage children, Robert Arthur and Natalie Wood, complicate matters. The boy falls in love with Jane and assumes that she feels the same about him, and the girl puts a strain on her father by getting herself expelled from various boarding schools. Crosby works his charms on Ethel Barrymore, the governess of a select school, and gets his daughter accepted. The boy is even more of a problem, because he wants to follow in his father's footsteps and write songs. He writes a song called "Call Me Tonight," which Bing at first sloughs off but later comes to realize has real quality. He also realizes he has ignored his kids for the past ten years, and he takes them on a vacation in the mountains.

The hit song of *Just for You* is the jaunty "Zing a Little Zong," sung by Crosby and Wyman. As a solo Jane sings "Checkin' My Heart," and later, in a big production number choreographed by Helen Tamiris, she leads a group of dancers and singers in a Latin number about a bullfighter and his loved one, "The Maiden of Guadalupe," sumptuously color photographed by George Barnes in a rich Mexican motif.

In the quaint lit-tle town of Guad-a-lu-pe there once lived a maid-en sweet and shy;

"The Maiden of Guadalupe" is not the only Latin song in *Just for You*. Bing Crosby had done well over the years with Latin American numbers, particularly one called "Bahia," and an attempt was made here to give him another hit along the same lines. In the context of the

Just For You: Bing Crosby, as a Broadway composer-producer, showing his cast how he wants "The Maiden of Guadalupe" delivered.

Just For You: Jane Wyman and Bing Crosby giving out with "Zing a Little Zong."

Just for You: Bing Crosby criticizing a song written by his son, Robert Arthur.

story Crosby explains to his production company how he wants the song staged and performed. Here the Latin beat is a samba, and the style is saucy and modernistic:

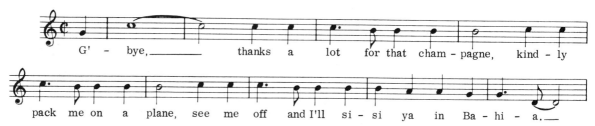

G' - bye,_____ thanks a lot for that cham - pagne, kind - ly pack me on a plane, see me off and I'll si - si ya in Ba - hi - a._____

Just for You, one of the last movie musicals made in Hollywood using an original screenplay, is also one of the most literate and witty. The abundant songs rise effortlessly from the running time of 104 minutes, a tribute to Nugent's direction. Jane Wyman, who seldom had an opportunity to reveal her pleasant singing voice during her years of stardom, is charming and amusing in this picture, doing several songs with Bing and a few as solos, including "He's Just Crazy for Me." Bing sings the philosophical "The Live Oak Tree" and shines in "On the Ten Ten, from Ten-Ten-Tennessee," a pleasing old song-and-dance number with Ben Lessey. The Crosby voice was in the peak of condition, and of the songs Warren and Robin wrote for him, "A Flight of Fancy" was obviously tailor-made for that rich, smooth baritone:

Could be_____ a flight of fan - cy;_____ Or was it you I kissed and held un - til the dawn?_____

Just for You: Bing Crosby and Ben Lessy performing "On the Ten-Ten From Ten-Ten-Tennessee."

THE CADDY (1953)

Harry Warren had no contract with Paramount while he worked there. He worked on a picture-to-picture arrangement that existed primarily because of Jerry Lewis, who had long admired Warren and wanted him for most of the pictures he did in the fifties.

Lewis asked Warren to come and see him and talk about writing songs for *The Caddy*. Lewis, it should be known, was the business partner, and Dean Martin was the retiring one—a situation that would soon end when Martin elected to make his own way.

The question of a lyricist came up, and Lewis suggested Jack Brooks, a man with a considerable background as a pianist-accompanist and a writer of nightclub songs and skits for Las Vegas performers. Brooks had written some of the lyrics to "You, Wonderful You" in *Summer Stock*, but after Warren was off the picture. At the mention of Brooks's name, Warren shrugged and admitted that he knew nothing of the man or his methods. Lewis suggested that they try a collaboration and that if it didn't work out, he would arrange for another lyricist. No further arrangement proved necessary, and Warren and Brooks became the Paramount songwriting team of the fifties.

Signing his contract to write songs for *The Caddy* brought Warren under the wing of executive producer Hal B. Wallis, who had discovered Martin and Lewis and made a film-comedy team of them. Says Warren, "Wallis had changed quite a lot from his days at Warners. Perhaps it was because he was in charge of his production company and not working for Warners, but he seemed much more affable and less dictatorial. There were no problems."

The Caddy consists mostly of flashbacks. It begins with Martin and Lewis appearing on stage at New York's Paramount Theatre, to the approval of hordes of fans, virtually portraying themselves. They sing and dance a sprightly patter song that would soon prove falsely prophetic, "What Would You Do without Me?" in which Jerry predicts that Dean wouldn't be able to survive:

After the opening song, Joseph Calleia, as Dean's father, tells the audience how their success came about, how they had started out as professional golfers and become a team when the timid Jerry backed away from competition and chose to become Dean's caddy and manager. The conceited Martin had become a big success on the greens and begun to feel as if he were sitting on top of the world. The song "It's a Whistlin' Kinda Morning" expresses his confidence:

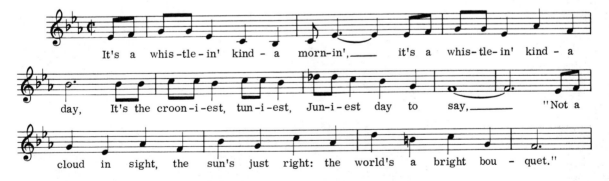

The Caddy: Dean Martin and Jerry Lewis singing "What Wouldja Do Without Me?"—the answer to which turned out to be "very well," in both cases.

The Caddy: Barbara Bates, Jerry Lewis, Dean Martin and Argentina Brunetti singing "That's Amore."

On the set of *The Caddy*: Dean Martin, lyricist Jack Brooks, producer Paul Jones and Jerry Lewis. Sitting: director Norman Taurog and Harry Warren.

The Caddy has a slight plot, just enough to support the misadventures of the two stars, their constant banter, and a half dozen songs. Martin becomes so swellheaded as a golfer that he tries to dispose of Lewis. Their troubles culminate in a squabble at Pebble Beach, developing into a riot that results in their being evicted from the world of golf. They take to show business as a last resort and, still bickering, end up at the Palace. Lewis has one big musical solo, his romp as a Boyer-ish lover, "The Gay Continental," and Martin informs his girlfriend, Donna Reed, that "It Takes a Lot of Little Likes to Make One Big Love."

The hit song from *The Caddy*—and the only song to emerge from any Martin-and-Lewis picture—is the lilting "That's Amore." The setting of the song is an Italian-immigrant, fisherfolk community in San Francisco. Martin takes Lewis there to meet his comic-stereotype family. Father Calleia, mother Argentina Brunette, and sister Barbara Bates all join Dean as he breaks into this humorous mock-Italian song. Recalls Warren, "What they were going to use was some traditional Italian song like 'Oh, Marie.' Brooks and I thought this was a wasted opportunity, and we prevailed upon Martin and Lewis to let us try something new. If they didn't like it they didn't have to use it. We didn't have any trouble with 'That's Amore,' and it became a smash seller for Dean."

If "That's Amore" had not been written, the song that would have been the most popular from the score is the love ballad "You're the Right One," crooned by Martin in his lazy style. He recorded it, and it did fairly well, but "That's Amore" stole the spotlight.

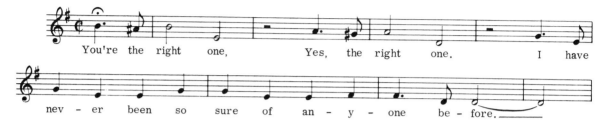

You're the right one, Yes, the right one. I have

nev - er been so sure of an - y - one be - fore.

ARTISTS AND MODELS (1955)

After completing his score for *The Caddy*, Harry Warren found out for the first time in his Hollywood experience what it was like to go without a project. In the twenty-three years since he had arrived to do *42nd Street* he had never stopped working. Now there were no more musicals, and only occasionally did a film call for a song or two, with a wide choice of composers to write them. Wages and fees fluctuated in this period, but Warren refused to reduce his price. Eighteen months went by, and he received another call from Paramount to come to the studio and discuss the scoring of a Martin-and-Lewis picture. The pair had made four other films since *The Caddy*, and the studio felt that it was time for another one with an extensive use of songs. The result was *Artists and Models*, a better-than-average vehicle for Martin and Lewis, greatly aided by its music.

The story has to do with the comic-book business. Martin is an artist, and Lewis is a would-be writer of children's stories. They live together in a New York garret, wondering where their next dollar will come from. This setting produces a pleasant song, as the pair imagine the food and the comforts they don't have:

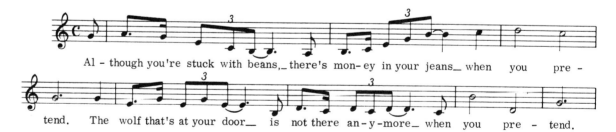

Al - though you're stuck with beans,_ there's mon-ey in your jeans_ when you pre -

tend. The wolf that's at your door_ is not there an-y-more_ when you pre - tend.

Success comes to the impecunious pair when Lewis starts dreaming aloud and coming up with lurid, fantastic tales in his sleep. Martin steals them and sells them to a publisher. Money changes the boys' life-style and provokes "The Lucky Song." Now Martin, back to his Lothario stance, woos artist Dorothy Malone with a flippant ditty, "You Look So Familiar." Success also enables them to meet a number of stunning girls, including Eva Gabor, Anita Ekberg, and Shirley MacLaine, who here made her second screen appearance.

Artists and Models: At the artists' ball, Martin and Lewis add some finishing touches to Anita Ekberg, who really doesn't need any.

Artists and Models: Shirley MacLaine, Jerry Lewis,
Dorothy Malone and Dean Martin.

The capricious Shirley appears to advantage in *Artists and Models*, clowning, singing, and dancing to the song "The Bat Lady." She also joins the entire cast for the artists'-ball finale.

Of the six songs by Warren and Jack Brooks the one that became popular was the love ballad "Inamorata," which is used in the picture both as a straight romantic song by Martin and as the background for a comedy dance by Martin and MacLaine on a staircase.

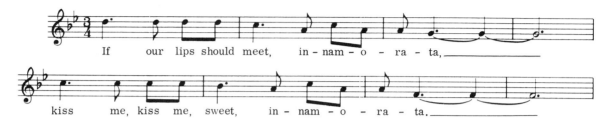

If our lips should meet, in - nam - o - ra - ta,___

kiss me, kiss me, sweet, in - nam - o - ra - ta.___

Dean Martin recorded this song, and it did well for him, but Warren recalls that Dean at first resisted the song, apparently because he was not then in favor of playing up his Italian heritage. Ironically, the success of the song, particularly in Italy, led to the ethnic image that Martin would capitalize upon.

Artists and Models was the sixteenth Martin-and-Lewis film, and there would be only two others before the team split up. Says Warren, "As far as I could see they kept their problems to themselves. I went to all the recording sessions, and they kidded around a lot. Perhaps the kidding was more in earnest than we realized, but you could sense a split was on the way.

"Jerry was always hyperactive. He was interested in every aspect of the business, and he wanted to have his say at every point. He was very talented, but there was a compulsiveness about him that people found draining.

"Dean was the opposite. I think he felt he was being shunted aside. He was very quiet and seemed to retreat to his dressing room all the time. When they split, the general feeling around the studio was that he would have a tough time making his way without Lewis, but that didn't turn out to be the case."

After they had finished their songs for *Artists and Models*, Paramount asked Warren and Brooks to write a song for their production of *The Rose Tattoo*, starring Burt Lancaster and Anna Magnani. With Magnani as an Italian widow in the United States, resisting virile Burt, the songwriters came up with a sultry song with an Italian flavor. But Alex North, who composed the incidental score, refused to use it in the picture, and the song had to rely for its popularity on its recordings by people like Perry Como and Percy Faith.

Warren's greatest song success of 1955 is strangely unidentified with his name. With lyricist Harold Adamson he wrote the theme song for the television series *The Legend of Wyatt Earp*, starring Hugh O'Brien. The series became one of the most profitable of its kind, and Warren's melody was, and still is, practically a household tune:

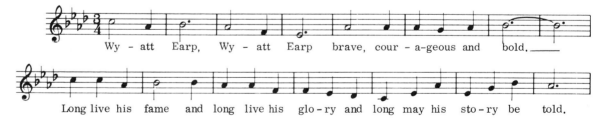

Wy - att Earp, Wy - att Earp brave, cour - a-geous and bold.___

Long live his fame and long live his glo - ry and long may his sto - ry be told.

Shortly after this, Warren was lucky with another title song. Producer Harold Hecht, a neighbor of Warren's, had just made the small-budget and rather offbeat *Marty*, which would bring Ernest Borgnine an Oscar for playing a plain working man. Paddy Chayefsky had

The Birds and the Bees: George Gobel and Mitzi Gaynor doing the title song.

The Birds and the Bees: Mitzi Gaynor vamping it up with "La Parisienne."

written the screenplay from his original television script and he prepared a simple lyric for Warren, who came up with a happy, dance-like melody to express Marty's feelings at the end of the picture when he finds the new way of life that takes him from loneliness to the companionship of a loving girl:

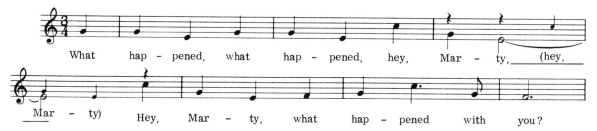

THE BIRDS AND THE BEES (1956)

Paramount took a chance on transferring television comic George Gobel to the big screen, but after two attempts, *The Birds and the Bees* and *I Married a Woman*, they decided that his wistful humor did not transfer with sufficient profit. The first film was a remake of Preston Sturges' classic *The Lady Eve*, with Gobel doing the Henry Fonda part of a woman-avoiding millionaire hunter on his way back to the United States from an African safari. As Eve, the lady who bags the hunter, Barbara Stanwyck had done the original, and the comely Mitzi Gaynor did the new version.

This considerable difference in the images of the actors required a different approach. Sturges worked with Sidney Sheldon on the rewrite and Norman Taurog directed, for a more obvious kind of humor—less subtle and more slapstick than the original. The decision was also made to add music, and Harry Warren was offered the job. He and lyricist Mack David came up with three songs, one of which was not used. The amount of music in a picture made no difference to Warren's fee. Whether it was two songs or six he was paid the same—the difference came with the royalties.

The songs give *The Birds and the Bees* a much-needed lift. Gobel was not enough of an actor to handle a long characterization, and his singing of the title song helps make his playing of the quietly eccentric hunter more amusing than it might otherwise have been. In fact, critics and film buffs met the film with near contempt, although it did well enough with the Gobel fans to cover its costs.

The role of the girl was altered somewhat; in the original Stanwyck had pretended to be an English lady after being found out as a cardsharp and rejected by Fonda. The device is similar here, except that Gaynor is required to be less mercenary, and when she decides to recapture Gobel she does it as a French vamp-entertainer. This allows for her saucy performance of the song "La Parisienne." With this and other ploys the female triumph over the male becomes simply a matter of time. Perhaps the best thing about *The Birds and the Bees* is the title song, sung and strutted by Gobel and Gaynor in a pleasing clap-hands beat:

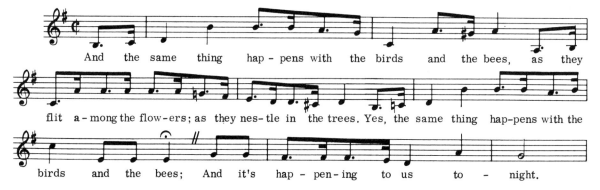

1956 was the year of Harry Warren's sharpest professional disappointment. All through the years of his activity at the studios he had received offers to write for the Broadway musical theater, an outlet that interested him much more than films, but he had never been free to accept.

In 1953 playwright-lyricists Jerome Lawrence and Robert Lee asked him to do a musical version of James Hilton's *Lost Horizon*. Hilton agreed to this and met with the songwriters at Warren's house in Beverly Hills, but before Warren could do much work on the project, Hilton died. Warren, Lawrence and Lee thought they should continue, but almost three years passed before the book and the music would see a Broadway stage. With Lew Ayres playing the part made famous by Ronald Colman, *Shangri-La* opened on June 13, 1956 and closed three weeks later.

Says Warren, "The fact that we opened during a heat wave and a subway strike didn't help, but I had sensed at the Philadelphia try-out that we were in trouble. The peculiar thing is that we had no problems raising money for it—in fact, we took in so much backing capital that we gave some of it back.

"As an audition it was a charming production. It was so intimate in a room with someone telling the story and the singers doing the songs that everyone thought we had a smash. But something happened to it when it went on stage with a big set; it lost its appeal—and I lost an opportunity I'd wanted for years. Like it or not, I was stuck with my Hollywood tag."

AN AFFAIR TO REMEMBER (1957)

Remakes have always been a fact of Hollywood life, but seldom are they done by the people who did the originals. Leo McCarey made *Love Affair* in 1939, with Charles Boyer and Irene Dunne, directing from a script he had written with Delmer Daves. He liked the picture so much that he felt compelled to make it again. He arranged with Twentieth Century–Fox and producer Jerry Wald to buy the property from Columbia, but found that they couldn't use the original title. This was not discovered until after Harry Warren and his lyricists, Harold Adamson and McCarey, had completed the song, causing some dexterous alterations in the song to accommodate the new title.

The song, sung over the main title by Vic Damone, is deceptively simple in construction. As if often the case with seemingly effortless pieces of music, it took more than the usual amount

An Affair to Remember: Cathleen Nesbitt and Deborah Kerr performing the title song.

An Affair to Remember: Director Leo McCarey, Cary Grant, lyricist Harold Adamson, Deborah Kerr and Harry Warren going over the title song.

of digging on Warren's part to write something that could serve the dramatic purpose of the film and yet find a life of its own as a popular song, which it most certainly did.

An Affair to Remember is a soap opera done with high style, expertly played by Cary Grant and Deborah Kerr and backed with all kinds of cinematic expertise, including superb color photography by Milton Krasner. McCarey was a filmmaker of exceptionally good taste, and he also had a great interest in music. This made working on the picture one of Harry Warren's most agreeable experiences in Hollywood.

McCarey wanted to be responsible for the lyrics on all the songs, but Warren advised him to bring in Harold Adamson, since McCarey would doubtless be very busy putting the project together and directing it. The credit on the four songs—a fifth was written but not used—is shared by Adamson and McCarey, but it is a fair assumption that the lion's share of the credit belongs to the adroit Adamson.

The story involves Grant and Kerr as passengers on a ship sailing from Naples to New York. They fall in love even though they have made romantic commitments elsewhere. Grant, a playboyish painter, takes Deborah to meet his aunt, Cathleen Nesbitt, when the boat docks at Villefranche. The refined old lady takes a liking to Deborah and plays for her an old French *chanson*—"An Affair to Remember" with a French lyric by Tanis Chandler—and it becomes the theme song of the lovers.

By the time they arrive in New York they are deeply in love, but to be sure that it is more than merely a shipboard romance, they agree to part for six months and then rendezvous at the top of the Empire State Building. When the time comes, Deborah is so eager to get there that she runs into the path of a taxi and is severely injured. Grant waits in vain and assumes she has lost interest.

308

Deborah is hospitalized for a long period and after recovering takes up teaching at a school. McCarey uses both the hospital sequence and the school setting as springboards for songs. McCarey, a devout Catholic who liked to include church sequences in his pictures, as he does here with Deborah praying in a chapel, also liked directing children and hearing them sing. In the hospital Deborah leads a group of children in singing the optimistic "Tomorrow Land," and in school she conducts "The Tiny Scout," a ditty about honor and conscience.

At one point the lovesick Grant visits Villefranche after his aunt has died, and as he stands in the empty living room he hears in his thoughts the echo of the song as it was previously played and sung. What he does not know is that Deborah feels the same way about him.

Their coming together again is skillfully protracted by McCarey. It comes about when Grant, now a successful painter, see a painting of her and through an art dealer manages to get information that leads him to her.

Most critics rushed to point out that *An Affair to Remember* was saccharine and not as good as McCarey's original. However, Twentieth Century–Fox had no cause to share their reservations.

What makes this version more interesting than the original is the use of music. Marni Nixon dubbed Deborah Kerr's singing voice, as she had the year before in *The King and I*. In both cases she did it with such skill, approximating Kerr's refined British accent and soft speaking voice, that the public was hardly aware of the dubbing. The musical score was composed by Hugo Friedhofer, one of the most respected of film scorers. Friedhofer, who won an Oscar for his *The Best Years of Our Lives*, had first met Warren at Warners in the late thirties but this was the only time the two men had the opportunity to work together.

Friedhofer used the Warren song as thematic material in his score, and in looking back on the job he says, "I was lucky with that one. Some of the title songs we have forced upon us aren't really worth using, but Harry's melody was a beautiful, flexible thing. My only fear was that the producers, a notoriously tin-eared lot, might be led to think this kind of treatment could be given songs of much less quality. However, with Harry Warren we were dealing with one of the most talented songwriters it has been our good fortune to have in the picture business."

Warren speaks kindly of Leo McCarey: "He was a musically sensitive person, and when you're working on a picture like this one that's half the battle won. So much of the time you're auditioning songs for people who are quite unmusical. Many of these movie executives seem to think their job calls for them to say no to everything. Maybe it makes them feel more secure. I wish there had been more men like McCarey."

Rock-a-Bye Baby: Jerry Lewis and babies.

309

ROCK-A-BYE BABY (1958)

Rock-a-bye Baby is a little less frenetic than most Jerry Lewis pictures of this period, leaning heavily on sentiment and putting Lewis in strangely maternal light. It is also his strongest bid to establish himself as a singer. Perhaps he broke away from Dean Martin partly to prove that he could handle songs in a straight as well as lunatic manner, but to his credit Lewis is notably fond of music and has an acceptable singing voice.

For all that, the public was not prepared to accept him as a crooner. As the producer of *Rock-a-bye Baby* he was in a position to allow himself most of the singing in this picture, which opens with his singing the title song and then, shortly after, singing "The Land of La La La," while wandering around a park in a musing mood:

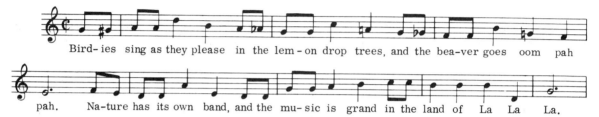

Bird-ies sing as they please in the lem-on drop trees, and the bea-ver goes oom pah pah. Na-ture has its own band, and the mu-sic is grand in the land of La La La.

Frank Tashlin wrote the script and directed the film.

Harry Warren wrote the six songs for *Rock-a-bye Baby*, working for the first time with the veteran Sammy Cahn, about whom Warren says, "He's the fastest and most facile lyricist I've

Rock-a-Bye Baby: Marilyn Maxwell doing "The White Virgin of the Nile."

ever come across. Sammy's method is to work with the composer in the same room, rather than going away and coming back later with the words, which is mostly what I had been used to. He's a humorous man and he loves performing his own songs, and he's a great socializer in show-business circles—just about the opposite of me.

"When we were doing these songs I was amazed at his speed. Sammy would have the title before I had finished the first eight measures of the melody and a complete lyric in what seemed no time at all." However, despite all this ease of operation none of the six songs, pleasant though they are, had any life beyond the run of the picture.

Lewis portrays a small-town TV-repair man whose childhood sweetheart has grown up to be a movie star, in the exciting shape of Marilyn Maxwell. She marries a Mexican bullfighter, but he is killed shortly after, and she ends up with triplets. She persuades Lewis to care for the children while she goes to Egypt to make a film called *The White Virgin of the Nile*, which is also the title of the song she sings during a production sequence.

The softhearted Lewis takes to the chores of motherhood with tender dedication, while still mooning about Marilyn. This unrequited love provokes him to sing a very gentle ballad, "Love is a Lonely Thing":

When you love in vain, love is a lone - ly thing.____

Like an end - less chain, you keep re - mem - ber - ing____

Also on hand are Marilyn's proud Italian father, played by ex-opera basso Salvatore Baccaloni, and young Connie Stevens as her sister, who loves Lewis, although he is too blind to realize it. This situation is a definite song cue and she sings "Why Can't He Care for Me?" Eventually he does, and their marriage produces quintuplets, more than compensating for the loss of the triplets when Marilyn arrives home.

Rock-a-bye Baby is amusing, although heavily dependent on a taste for Jerry Lewis and a tolerance for humor dealing with the problems of infancy. The pity is that Lewis decided to indulge himself in the singing department. The only great voice in the picture belongs to Baccaloni, who had to be content with sharing a duet with Lewis. This occurs as the two of them sing a lullaby to the triplets. With a title like "Dormi, Dormi, Dormi," it would have been much better as a solo by Baccaloni. The Warren melody is very much in the mode of an old Italian lullaby:

CINDERFELLA (1960)

In turning "Cinderella" into a picture starring himself, Jerry Lewis, who produced it, again turned to Harry Warren to come up with the music. This also brought Warren together again with Jack Brooks after a gap of five years. Brooks, who died in 1971, at fifty-nine, may not have been a great lyricist, but his background in the entertainment business and his facility with music made him an easy collaborator. Frank Tashlin both wrote the script and directed it, and among his other talents he had the ability to handle the superenergetic Jerry.

The plot follows the traditional line, except that the male and female parts are switched. Lewis is treated badly by his stepmother, Judith Anderson, who favors her spoiled, nasty sons, Henry Silva and Robert Hutton. Ed Wynn is the whimsical fairy godfather who takes pity on the downtrodden Jerry and uses his magic wand to bring Jerry some happiness. The beautiful loved one is a visiting foreign princess, Anna Maria Alberghetti, and the band playing at the

CinderFella: Jerry Lewis and Fairy Godfather Ed Wynn.

312

The Ladies Man: Jerry Lewis and a wildly balletic moment.

ball in her honor is conducted by none other than Count Basie. Lewis's characterization of CinderFella is marked by feelings of inferiority and humility, expressed in the song "Let Me Be a People:"

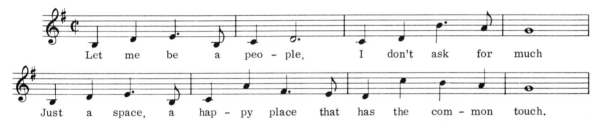

Let me be a peo - ple, I don't ask for much

Just a space, a hap - py place that has the com - mon touch.

Lewis overdoes the "common touch" mentioned in Brooks's lyrics. He desires to be a "people" because he considers persons to be those who take themselves too seriously and become pompous. At the conclusion of this Lewis account of the fable, the princess comes down to his level and renounces refinement to spend her life with him.

This film was perhaps an odd choice for Lewis, but at this point in his career none of his enterprises lost money. *CinderFella* might best have been done entirely in song. Instead, two of the Warren songs were dropped, although one of them, the charming "Turn It on," does appear on the LP album Lewis made for the Dot label. "The Princess Waltz" was a collaboration between Warren and Walter Scharf, who composed the incidental score and conducted the music for the picture.

Warren has always felt that what Jerry Lewis wanted most of all in the way of music was a hit song, perhaps so he could thumb his nose at Dean Martin. But the public never accepted. Lewis as a singer, and Warren was never able to come up with a hit for him. The nearest to a hit in *CinderFella* is a gentle song about the need for love:

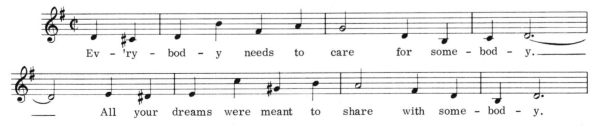

Ev - 'ry - bod - y needs to care for some - bod - y.____

____ All your dreams were meant to share with some - bod - y.

313

THE LADIES' MAN (1961)

Harry Warren's third picture for Jerry Lewis proved to be the last film for which he would be hired. There would be offers to write title songs, but this was the last picture requiring Warren songs as part of the story line. Jack Brooks was also hired as a lyricist but he and Warren had to come up with only two songs, neither of which received much attention from the public. In previous times these songs might have become popular but in 1961, with most disc jockeys promoting noise, there was little hope for ballads with pretty melodies.

The Ladies' Man also pleased few people other than the regular Lewis fans. This time Jerry chose both to produce and to direct the film, as well as writing the screenplay with Bill Richmond. More than one critic pointed out that what the talented Lewis needed most of all was a strong restraining hand, preferably belonging to someone else.

Here Jerry is a timid houseboy in a Hollywood boardinghouse run by ex-opera star Helen Traubel, who is heard singing in only one short sequence. Lewis doesn't like girls because of an early unhappy love affair. This theme provides the fun as all thirty-one young beauties in the boardinghouse cause him sundry embarrassments. One of the more amusing moments arises from a hallucination in which he ballet dances preposterously to the music of Harry James.

In an appealingly lighthearted moment, Jerry and the girls sing "Don't Go to Paris." The song warns about Paris's aura of romance.

Romance comes to Jerry in the agreable shape of Pat Stanley, who has the drawn-out problem of getting Jerry to realize that he needs love, that he is capable of experiencing it, and that she is the one to bring it to him. In another picture this delightful little song might have won more attention:

The music director of this and the other Lewis pictures for which Warren wrote the songs was Walter Scharf. He had first met Warren in the late thirties at Warners when Scharf was employed as an arranger, and he also worked in that capacity on some of the Warren musicals at Fox. In time Scharf became one of Hollywood's leading composer-conductors. About his friend Harry Warren he says, "In the first place he's a magnificent man. As a songwriter he is unique because he has written over such a long course of time, and at no time has he ever written anything less than quality. This is incredible for a man with so little formal musical education. His education has come from his own study—and his love of music is such that he has never stopped studying it. The mystery of music has never lost its fascination for him.

"To me he exemplifies, more than any other songwriter we have ever had, the complete understanding of songwriting as a popular art—an art as it can be digested by the public.

314

Ship To:

Barbara L. Favia
34 BUNKER BLVD
PALMYRA, VIRGINIA 22963-2501

Order ID: 113-6267978-8136209

Thank you for buying from CathbertFarmsNC on Amazon Marketplace.

Shipping Address:
Barbara L. Favia
34 BUNKER BLVD
PALMYRA, VIRGINIA 22963-2501

	Order Date:	Jun 30, 2014
	Shipping Service:	Standard
	Buyer Name:	Barbara L. Favia
	Seller Name:	CathbertFarmsNC

Quantity	Product Details
1	**The Hollywood Musical: The Saga of Songwriter Harry Warren [Paperback] [1987] Tony Thomas; Bing Crosby** **SKU:** TN-ADA-FF2G **ASIN:** 0806510668 **Listing ID:** 0323MAPLX2A **Order Item ID:** 30641382959506 **Condition:** Used - Very Good **Comments:** softcover ....slight wear on cover .....SHIPS IN A CORRUGATED BOX WITH USPS DELIVERY TRACKING

Returning your item:
Go to "Your Account" on Amazon.com, click "Your Orders" and then click the "seller profile" link for this order to get information about the return and refund policies that apply.
Visit http://www.amazon.com/returns to print a return shipping label. Please have your order ID ready.

Thanks for buying on Amazon Marketplace. To provide feedback for the seller please visit www.amazon.com/feedback. To contact the seller, please visit Amazon.com and click on "Your Account" at the top of any page. In Your Account, go to the "Orders" section and click on the link "Leave seller feedback". Select the order or click on the "View Order" button. Click on the "seller profile" under the appropriate product. On the lower right side of the page under "Seller Help", click on "Contact this seller".

"Warren was always able to touch the public nerve. He touched it constantly. He developed, he kept pace, he kept going, and his ear was always attuned to better music.

"And I've never known a more disciplined songwriter. His work habits are impeccable, and it was never necessary to question any music than he handed in. What he gave us was what we used, and only someone working in this profession can really appreciate that."

The Ladies' Man is not much of an ending for a career as long, prolific, and distinguished as Harry Warren's. Looking back to 1961, Warren says, "I had no idea that would be the end of it. As always, I thought something would come up, but nothing did. I had been so used to being called in to do pictures that it was hard to realize the business was all over. There were a few calls from time to time to discuss my availability for odd songs here and there. Many times these things would fall through, and sometimes they wouldn't even bother to let you know. The standard of manners on the production level isn't very high. In '62 Leo McCarey called me to write a title song for his picture *Satan Never Sleeps*. Again Harold Adamson did most of the

The Ladies Man: Jerry Lewis and Pat Stanley stepping out to the music of Harry James and his Band.

At the Cairo airport in 1956, to make a movie that never came to be: Mrs. Josephine Warren, lyricist Ralph Blane, Harry Warren, producer John Shelton, Busby Berkeley and an Eqyptian minister.

315

At his eightieth birthday party, with his family: daughter Joan (Cookie), grandchildren Peter and Jophe, Harry Warren, grandson Jeffrey, Mrs. Warren and granddaughter Julia. Not in the picture is the youngest grandson, John Paul.

316

Erwin Drake, the President of the American Guild of Authors and Composers presents a plaque to Harry Warren on the occasion of the AGAC party to mark Warren's eightieth birthday.

lyrics with Leo, but it was a waste of time. It's almost impossible to write a song called 'Satan Never Sleeps' and expect the public to buy it."

Warren was associated with Leo McCarey and Harold Adamson on a major disappointment for all of them. McCarey, who died in 1969, had long wanted to do a musical based on the career of Marco Polo. He raised the preproduction money and commissioned Warren and Adamson to write the song. The idea was to make the picture in Spain, with Spanish financing, but after months of haggling and hoping the project fell through when the money failed to materialize. Warren's songs for this project constitute his only unpublished and unperformed score.

A similar experience came his way soon after that when ex-actor John Shelton hired Warren, lyricist Ralph Blane, and Busby Berkeley, who would direct, to make a movie musical in Egypt. Its title, *Only the Poor Dream Rich*, proved somewhat prophetic when the Egyptians failed to come up with the promised backing. Fortunately, Warren had held back on writing the score.

Another factor that contributed to the decline of Hollywood songwriters was the use of title songs. This had come about when the producers realized that a good title song was the best and least expensive means of promotion possible. Dimitri Tiomkin had started the trend almost single-handedly when he wrote the song for *High Noon* in 1952.

The producers' reasoning could hardly have been more commercial—title songs benefited movie producers, publishers, record companies, radio stations, and singers. But there were two adverse effects—the use of title songs in this way tended to lower the standard of dramatic music composition for films, because the producers looked for hit tunes and ignored the art of scoring; and most of the film composers wanted to write their own title songs. In many cases this met with the producers' approval because it meant they could get title songs at no extra charge, without having to hire songwriters.

A case in point is *Separate Tables* in 1958. Producer Harold Hecht commissioned Warren to write a theme song, with lyrics by Harold Adamson, but he also hired David Raksin to compose and conduct the incidental score. The difference in musical style between Warren and Raksin is vast. Raksin objected to using the Warren melody and proceeded to write his own title music. This met with justifiable anger from Warren, who felt that he had provided a song

317

that would be of benefit to the picture. When they appealed to the producers, Raksin lost the point. The Warren song, sung by Vic Damone, was heard over the credits of the picture, although Raksin still refused to use the Warren melody in the body of his score. Warren afterward resigned from the Screen Composers' Guild, feeling that the membership was biased toward composers, rather than established songwriters, being hired to write theme songs.

Situations like this have arisen all too frequently in Hollywood; they could be avoided if the producers were more astute and tactful in hiring and handling talent. Both Warren and Raksin feel they were put in an unnecessary and unethical position.

Be that as it may, what Warren thought *Separate Tables* needed was a gentle, slightly bittersweet love song:

Sep'-rate ta - bles, two lone - ly peo - ple sit at sep' - rate ta - bles

Later that year Warren and Ned Washington wrote another title song, this one for the Western *These Thousand Hills*, but nothing came of it. Says Warren, "There have been too many cases where title songs were forced on pictures that didn't need them. This was one of them, and I'd rather forget it."

Harry Warren's only song for a movie since *Satan Never Sleeps* has been a title piece for Universal's *Rosie*, a 1968 madcap comedy starring Rosalind Russell. It occurred to the producers to bring Warren together with Johnny Mercer for this one:

How d' ya like_ our Ro - sie? Is that a fa - bu-lous doll?____

The film did poorly, and little came of the song, except for Louis Armstrong's recording.

Warren's output since then has been very slim. He has written a mass, but it uses a Latin text, and with the current use of English in the Catholic church, it seems unlikely that the work will be performed. He has written a few odd songs, mostly with friends, but none has approached being a hit.

Says Warren, "Perhaps only another songwriter would understand this, but you can't sit down and write hits. You're lucky if you get one hit in writing twenty songs. I did well in the past because circumstances forced me to be productive. For twenty-five years in Hollywood I had my nose to the grindstone. I thought about music all the time—hardly a day passed when I wasn't thinking about ideas for melodies and sitting at the piano digging them out. There are no rules for writing songs, no secret formulas for composition. It's a God-given talent, and you have to work at it."

Harry Warren's association with the Hollywood studios deflated like a punctured balloon during the sixties. In this sad regard he was not alone—any experienced songwriter who stayed in California suffered the same fate. The market had both changed and shriveled. Television offered limited opportunities for the giants of American song, although it used their old songs continuously. The decline was also abetted by the ever-decreasing number of theaters in New York and the productions of fewer stage musicals. Escalating costs had made the musical production a considerable risk. The sixties were a far, far cry from the burgeoning days of the twenties, thirties, and forties.

The situation in the recording industry was also peculiar for men like Warren. Rarely was there any demand for new material from the famous songwriters, although their standards were constantly recorded for the older market, the so-called middle-brow trade.

Warren had no problem income—his royalties are still the envy of his peers. The problem was in no longer being asked to write anything new. Irving Berlin, Cole Porter, Hoagy Carmichael, Vernon Duke, Harold Arlen, Sammy Fain, Jimmy McHugh, and many others shared this dilemma. It was as if some huge, invisible hand had eased America's most famous songwriters to the sidelines. The move was deliberate; the profits from pop music, after the introduction of microgroove recordings and the proliferation of radio stations, came more and more from the youth market, with rock 'n' roll as its principal interest.

All the great American songwriters are uniform in expressing anger and regret over the decline in the standards of their craft since the early fifties. One of the most eloquent of these men is Arthur Schwartz, whose distinguished career as a composer for the theater began in the late twenties and whose output includes "Dancing in the Dark," "You and the Night and the Music," and "Something to Remember You By," all written with lyricist Howard Dietz. In recent years, Schwartz, who started his professional life as a lawyer, has devoted his legal and artistic talents to the guidance of ASCAP. He feels strongly that music has been debased in order to make huge profits.

Says Schwartz, "We feel that there has been a process of manipulation that the American public, and the rest of the world, has had imposed upon them by monetary influences, mainly in the broadcasting industry. In this period we have had music of admittedly inferior quality which has corrupted the taste of our youth. A great many of us composers are fighting hard to combat this monopoly. This worst music is a blight upon us and it would not have happened except for the commercial attitude of the broadcasting industry in America. It would not have been born and it would not have blossomed without a definite and continuous manipulation in the millions and millions of dollars."

Harry Warren's eightieth birthday was celebrated by a large party of family and friends at his home on December 24, 1973. The American Guild of Authors and Composers gave a belated eightieth-birthday salute on the following March 20. John Green was the master of

At the AGAC party, Harry Warren greets Nelson Riddle, following Riddle's playing of "You're My Everything" on the trombone.

319

Harry Warren died in Los Angeles on September 22, 1981 at age 87.

ceremonies, and most of Hollywood's colony of songwriters, conductors and composers turned up to pay their respects. Dozens of Warren songs were sung and played by his colleagues and the evening ended with all of them joining voices for "You Must Have Been a Beautiful Baby." Among the guests was arranger-orchestrator Eddie Powell, who had got his first major break at the age of twenty-one in New York arranging Warren's songs for *The Laugh Parade*, and who later worked on many of the Warren musicals at Twentieth Century-Fox.

Says Powell: "That night was a revelation. We had all of us known Harry most of our working lives but with about forty of us going up there and, good or bad, singing our favorite Warren songs, a kind of spell gradually came over the place. These were songs encompassing every mood and tempo in which a song can be written, and even though I'd long known all this music, it suddenly occurred to me how much style it had. The simplicity of his music, the natural gaiety and warmth, and the lack of pretense. You knew you always knew it, but that night you realized you were in the presence of a wonderboy. A genuine bit of magic."

Like so many so-called senior citizens, Harry Warren was forced into retirement long before he was ready for it. In fact, it is likely that Warren would never have retired. "I didn't want to stop," he says. "I liked writing music, and I enjoyed working. If they hadn't stopped making movie musicals I would probably have gone on. Provided you don't turn senile, age doesn't mean much in the arts. I've always felt I got better as I went along. This business of forcing people to retire at sixty-five is ridiculous. I've known people of that age who were at the peak of their capability. Why do we have to get rid of them?"

Warren's affable, easygoing personality masks a good deal of bitterness about the arbitrary ending of his career. He readily admits to being "old-fashioned," and he is adamant in his devotion to the time-tested concepts of melody, harmony, and rhythm. He is appalled by what he considers the lack of musical knowledge of many of the newer musicians in the pop field. "They write about three chords," he says. "They use a major chord and a seventh and then go back to the major chord—and they repeat the same words over and over. There's hardly any form to it. They say people like this stuff. Well, I think it's because the record companies have forced them to like it. It's too much for me. I can't figure it out."

Looking back on fifty years of writing music and some four hundred songs, Harry Warren is amazed by his own productivity. "I don't know how I did it," he says. "Every time I started to work on a movie I was afraid I wouldn't be able to come up with anything. But I kept digging, and up it came. I'm glad I achieved what I acheived, but don't ask me to explain it. If I hadn't had the talent for composing, I don't know what I would have done. Maybe I'd have been a streetcar conductor.

"The basic drive of my life has been my love of music, and if people have liked my music it has to be because it came from the heart. My only regret is that it hasn't brought me more personal recognition. My colleagues kid me about this, but it irritates me, as recently, when someone suggested to Warner Bros. Records that they put out an album of my songs and the executive to whom the suggestion was made asked, 'Who's he?' It gets a little irksome to hear myself referred to as America's greatest unknown songwriter. I've always avoided publicity, but I'd like to be known as the man who wrote my songs instead of hearing people say, 'Did he write *that*?'

As for my musical philosophy, I've always written music the way I felt it. I write for the public because I feel like the public, the way they would write if they could. You don't have to know anything about music to understand what I write. Mine are simple melodies. In music there are certain chords that are tender and poignant—it's the universal language."

Zing a Little Zong

Words by
LEO ROBIN

Music by
HARRY WARREN

That's Amore
(That's Love)

Words by
JACK BROOKS

Music by
HARRY WARREN

An Affair to Remember
(OUR LOVE AFFAIR)

Lyric by
HAROLD ADAMSON and LEO McCAREY
French Lyric by Tanis Chandler

Music by
HARRY WARREN

Moderately *(with movement)*

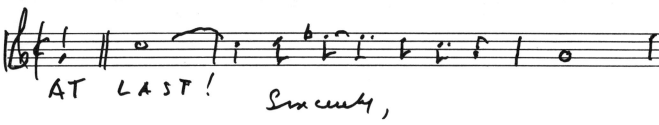

AT LAST!

Sincerely,

Harry Warren

PART SIX
THE HARRY WARREN CATALOG

Note: In this listing the name of the lyricist is given in parenthesis after the title of the song. The publishers listed are those holding the current copyrights on the songs.

1922

Rose of the Rio Grande (*Edgar Leslie*), Four Jays Music Inc., Mills Music Inc, and Edgar Leslie Music Inc.

1923

Home in Pasadena (*Edgar Leslie and G. Clarke*), Four Jays Music Inc., Mills Music Inc, and Edgar Leslie Music Inc.

So This Is Venice (*Edgar Leslie and G. Clarke*), Four Jays Music Inc., Mills Music Inc, and Edgar Leslie Music Inc.

Sweet Anita (*Ben Russell*), Leo Feist Inc.

I Don't Want That Kind of Love (*Ben Russell*), Leo Feist Inc.

1924

Oh! Eva (*Edgar Leslie and G. Clarke*), Four Jays Music Inc., Clarke and Leslie Inc.

Beau Brummel Joe (*Henry Creamer*), J. H. Remick and Co.

Stop Stutterin', Sam (*Henry Creamer*), Skidmore Music Co.

The Only, Only One (*J. V. Monaco and Bud Green*), Shapiro, Bernstein and Co.

Maybe You Will, Maybe You Won't (*Billy Rose and Mort Dixon*), Jack Mills Music Inc.

1925

Call Me Up When You're Lonesome (*Bud Green*), Shapiro, Bernstein Co.

Oh, How I Love Fannie (*Bud Green*), Shapiro, Bernstein Co.

Is Zat So? (*Buddy de Sylva and Robert King*), Shapiro, Bernstein Co.

Seminola (*Buddy de Sylva*), Skidmore Music Co., Inc.

She's the Sweetest Gal in Kankakee (*Bud Green*), Shapiro, Bernstein and Co.

Want a Little Lovin'? (*Benny Davis*), Shapiro, Bernstein and Co.

Way Down South in Chicago (*Henry Creamer, Bud Green, and C. Robinson*), Shapiro, Bernstein & Co.

The Runaway Train (*Robert Massey*), Shapiro, Bernstein & Co.

1926

In My Gondola (*Bud Green*), Shapiro, Bernstein & Co.

331

I'm Lonely (without You) (*Bud Green*), Shapiro, Bernstein & Co.

I Love My Baby (*Bud Green*), Shapiro, Bernstein & Co.

Wimmin—Ah! (*Bud Green*), Shapiro, Bernstein & Co.

You Can't Shush Katie (*Henry Creamer*), Shapiro, Bernstein & Co.

Tiger Baby (*Jo Trent*), Shapiro, Bernstein & Co.

You Gotta Know How to Love (*Bud Green*), Shapiro, Bernstein & Co.

A Little Girl, a Little Boy, a Little Moon (*Robert King*), Shapiro, Bernstein & Co.

Tommy Hawk (*Robert King and H. Johnson*), Shapiro, Bernstein & Co.

The Sphinx (*Robert King*), Shapiro, Bernstein & Co.

Too Many Kisses (*Billy Rose and Al Dubin*), Shapiro, Bernstein & Co.

Where Do You Work-a John? (*Weinberg and Marks*), Shapiro, Bernstein & Co.

Lilly (*B. MacDonald and M. Boones*), Shapiro, Bernstein & Co.

1927

My Regular Gal (*Bud Green*), Shapiro, Bernstein & Co.

Who's in Your Arms Tonight? (*Bud Cooper and Sam H. Stept*), Shapiro, Bernstein & Co.

One Sweet Letter from You (*S. Clare and L. Brown*), Shapiro, Bernstein & Co.

Clementine from New Orleans (*Henry Creamer*), Shapiro, Bernstein & Co.

Away Down South in Heaven (*Bud Green*), Shapiro, Bernstein & Co.

An' Furthermore (*Bud Green*), Shapiro, Bernstein & Co.

Are You in Love with Me? (*Al Piantadosi*), Shapiro, Bernstein & Co.

1928

Wob-a-ly Walk (*Bud Green*), Shapiro, Bernstein & Co.

Hello Montreal (*Billy Rose and Mort Dixon*), Irving Berlin Inc.

We Are in Society (*Mort Dixon*), J. H. Remick & Co.

What of It, We Love It (*Billy Rose and Mort Dixon*), Irving Berlin Inc.

One Little Kiss in the Moonlight (*Billy Rose and Mort Dixon*), Remick Music Corp.

Twelve o'Clock Waltz (*Billy Rose and Mort Dixon*), Remick Music Corp.

Two Lips (*Billy Rose and Mort Dixon*), Remick Music Corp.

Old Man Sunshine (*Billy Rose and Mort Dixon*), Remick Music Corp.

When I Tip Tip Toe Up a Tuck Tuck Tucky Lane (*Billy Rose and Mort Dixon*), DeSylva, Brown and Henderson Inc.

Then Came the Dawn (*Al Dubin*), Gene Austin, Inc.

Nagasaki (*Mort Dixon*), Remick Music Corp.

My Life Is in Your Hands (*Lewis and Young*), Remick Music Corp.

Weepin' Willow Weep No More (*Benny Davis*), Villa Moret, Inc.

When Eliza Rolls Her Eyes (*Gus Kahn*), Irving Berlin Inc.

Along Came Sweetness (*Mort Dixon*), Remick Music Corp.

Every Night in the Week (*Lewis and Young*), Remick Music Corp.

Mi Adado (The Wolf Song) (*Lewis and Young*), Famous Music Corp.

Cheerio Cheery Lips, Cheerio (*Mort Dixon*), Remick Music Corp.

Where the Shy Little Violets Grow (*Gus Kahn*), Remick Music Corp.

Won't You Tell Me, Hon, When We're Gonna Be One? (*Lewis and Young*), Remick Music Corp.

1929

What Didja Wanna Make Me Love You For? (*Mort Dixon*), Remick Music Corp.

Finding the Long Way Home (*Gus Kahn*), Remick Music Corp.

Here We Are (*Gus Kahn*), Remick Music Corp.

Where the Sweet Forget-Me-Nots Remember (*Mort Dixon*), Remick Music Corp.

Just a Little Glimpse of Paradise (*Bert Kalmar and Harry Ruby*), Remick Music Corp.

There Was Nothing Else to Do (*Bert Kalmar and Harry Ruby*), Remick Music Corp.

Poor Unlucky Me (*Mort Dixon*), Remick Music Corp.

When You're Seeing Sweetie Home (*Lewis and Young*), Remick Music Corp.

1930

SPRING IS HERE (*Film*):

Absence Makes the Heart Grow Fonder (*Lewis and Young*), Music Publishers Holding Corp.

Crying for the Carolinas (*Lewis and Young*), Music Publishers Holding Corp.

Have a Little Faith in Me (*Lewis and Young*), Music Publishers Holding Corp.

Bad Baby (*Lewis and Young*), Music Publishers Holding Corp.

How Shall I Tell? (*Lewis and Young*), Music Publishers Holding Corp.

What's the Big Idea? (*Lewis and Young*), Music Publishers Holding Corp.

Gid-ap Garibaldi (*Howard Johnson and Billy Moll*), Shapiro, Bernstein and Co.

I Remember You from Somewhere (*Edgar Leslie*), Crawford Music

Tellin' It to the Daisies (*Joe Young*), Music Publishers Holding Corp.

Wasting My Love on You (*Edgar Leslie*), Music Publishers Holding Corp.

Reminiscing (*Edgar Leslie*), Music Publishers Holding Corp.

How Are You Tonight in Hawaii? (*Edgar Leslie*), Music Publishers Holding Corp.

If You Can't Have the Girl of Your Dreams (*Joe Young*), Music Publishers Holding Corp.

SWEET AND LOW (*Stage production*):
Cheerful Little Earful (*Ira Gershwin and Billy Rose*), Music Publishers Holding Corp.

He's Not Worth Your Tears (*Mort Dixon and Billy Rose*), Music Publishers Holding Corp.

Would You Like to Take a Walk? (*Billy Rose and Mort Dixon*), Music Publishers Holding Corp.

The River and Me (*Al Dubin*), Music Publishers Holding Corp.

Cover a Clover with Kisses (*Mort Dixon*), Music Publishers Holding Corp.

What Good Is the Lane, If You Can't Have the Girl of Your Dreams? (*Mort Dixon*), Remick Music Inc.

Boo Hoo Hoo, Ha Ha Ha! (*Edgar Leslie*), Remick Music Inc.

Ma Mère (*Al Jolson and Irving Caesar*), Remick Music Inc.

1931

By the River Sainte Marie (*Edgar Leslie*), Robbins, Feist and Miller Music Inc.

When the Shepherd Leads His Flock Back Home (*Edgar Leslie*), Chappel and Co., Inc.

Gotta Go to Town (*Mort Dixon*), Harms, Inc.

CRAZY QUILT (*Stage production*):
Crazy Quilt (*Bud Green*), Music Publishers Holding Corp.

Sing a Little Jingle (*Mort Dixon*), Music Publishers Holding Corp.

In the Merry Month of Maybe (*Ira Gershwin and Billy Rose*), Music Publishers Holding Corp.

I Found a Million Dollar Baby (*Mort Dixon and Billy Rose*), Music Publishers Holding Corp.

THE LAUGH PARADE (*Stage production*):
The More You Hurt Me, the More You Make Me Care (*Mort Dixon and Joe Young*), Music Publishers Holding Corp.

You're My Everything (*Dixon and Young*), Music Publishers Holding Corp.

Ooh, That Kiss (*Dixon and Young*), Music Publishers Holding Corp.

The Torch Song (*Dixon and Young*), Music Publishers Holding Corp.

Love Me Forever (*Dixon and Young*), Music Publishers Holding Corp.

I Wish I Could Laugh at Love (*Dixon and Young*), Music Publishers Holding Corp.

1932

Deep in Your Eyes (*Mort Dixon*), Music Publishers Holding Corp.

Someone to Care For (*Gus Kahn*), Music Publishers Holding Corp.

A Great Big Bunch of You (*Mort Dixon*), Music Publishers Holding Corp.

Too Many Tears (*Al Dubin*), Music Publishers Holding Corp.

Come Home (*Ted Koehler*), Music Publishers Holding Corp.

I May Never Pass Your Way Again (*Irving Kahal*), Music Publishers Holding Corp.

THE CROONER (*Film*):
Three's a Crowd (*Irving Kahal*), Music Publishers Corp.

42ND STREET (*Film*):
42nd Street (*Al Dubin*), Music Publishers Holding Corp.

Shuffle Off to Buffalo (*Al Dubin*), Music Publishers Holding Corp.

Young and Healthy (*Al Dubin*), Music Publishers Holding Corp.

You're Getting to Be a Habit with Me (*Al Dubin*), Music Publishers Holding Corp.

It Must Be June (*Al Dubin*), Music Publishers Holding Corp.

1933

GOLD DIGGERS OF 1933 (*Film*):
Shadow Waltz (*Al Dubin*), Music Publishers Holding Corp.

We're in the Money (*Al Dubin*), Music Publishers Holding Corp.

Pettin' in the Park (*Al Dubin*), Music Publishers Holding Corp.

Remember My Forgotten Man (*Al Dubin*), Music Publishers Holding Corp.

I've Got to Sing a Torch Song (*Al Dubin*), Music Publishers Holding Corp.

ROMAN SCANDALS (*Film*):

Put a Tax on Love (*Al Dubin*), Music Publishers Holding Corp.

Rome Wasn't Built in a Day (*Al Dubin*), Music Publishers Holding Corp.

Keep Young and Beautiful (*Al Dubin*), Music Publishers Holding Corp.

Build a Little Home (*Al Dubin*), Music Publishers Holding Corp.

No More Love (*Al Dubin*), Music Publishers Holding Corp.

FOOTLIGHT PARADE (*Film*):

Honeymoon Hotel (*Al Dubin*), Music Publishers Holding Corp.

Shanghai Lil (*Al Dubin*), Music Publishers Holding Corp.

1934

MOULIN ROUGE (*Film*):

Song of Surrender (*Al Dubin*), Music Publishers Holding Corp.

The Boulevard of Broken Dreams (*Al Dubin*), Music Publishers Holding Corp.

Coffee in the Morning, Kisses in the Night (*Al Dubin*), Music Publishers Holding Corp.

TWENTY MILLION SWEETHEARTS (*Film*):

I'll String Along with You (*Al Dubin*), Music Publishers Holding Corp.

Fair and Warmer (*Al Dubin*), Music Publishers Holding Corp.

What Are Your Intentions? (*Al Dubin*), Music Publishers Holding Corp.

Out for No Good (*Al Dubin*), Music Publishers Holding Corp.

WONDER BAR (*Film*):

Wonder Bar (*Al Dubin*), Music Publishers Holding Corp.

Don't Say Goodnight (*Al Dubin*), Music Publishers Holding Corp.

Why Do I Dream Those Dreams? (*Al Dubin*), Music Publishers Holding Corp.

Vive la France (*Al Dubin*), Music Publishers Holding Corp.

Goin, to Heaven on a Mule (*Al Dubin*), Music Publishers Holding Corp.

DAMES (*Film*):

Dames (*Al Dubin*), Music Publishers Holding Corp.

I Only Have Eyes for You (*Al Dubin*), Music Publishers Holding Corp.

The Girl at the Ironing Board (*Al Dubin*), Music Publishers Holding Corp.

SWEET MUSIC (*Film*):

Sweet Music (*Al Dubin*), Music Publishers Holding Corp.

1935

LIVING ON VELVET (*Film*):

Living on Velvet (*Al Dubin*), Music Publishers Holding Corp.

GOLD DIGGERS OF 1935 (*Film*):

Lullaby of Broadway (*Al Dubin*), Music Publishers Holding Corp.

The Words Are in My Heart (*Al Dubin*), Music Publishers Holding Corp.

I'm Goin' Shopping with You (*Al Dubin*), Music Publishers Holding Corp.

Sweet and Slow (*Al Dubin*), Music Publishers Holding Corp.

GO INTO YOUR DANCE (*Film*):

Go into Your Dance (*Al Dubin*), Music Publishers Holding Corp.

Casino de Paree (*Al Dubin*), Music Publishers Holding Corp.

A Good Old-Fashioned Cocktail (*Al Dubin*), Music Publishers Holding Corp.

About a Quarter to Nine (*Al Dubin*), Music Publishers Holding Corp.

She's a Latin from Manhattan (*Al Dubin*), Music Publishers Holding Corp.

The Little Things You Used to Do (*Al Dubin*), Music Publishers Holding Corp.

Mammy, I'll Sing about You (*Al Dubin*), Music Publishers Holding Corp.

IN CALIENTE (*Film*):

Muchacha (*Al Dubin*), Music Publishers Holding Corp.

BROADWAY GONDOLIER (*Film*):

Lonely Gondolier (*Al Dubin*), Music Publishers Holding Corp.

The Pig and the Cow, and the Dog and the Cat (*Al Dubin*), Music Publishers Holding Corp.

Flagenheim's Odorless Cheese (*Al Dubin*), Music Publishers Holding Corp.

Outside of You (*Al Dubin*), Music Publishers Holding Corp.

You Can Be Kissed (*Al Dubin*), Music Publishers Holding Corp.

The Rose in Her Hair (*Al Dubin*), Music Publishers Corp.

Lulu's Back in Town (*Al Dubin*), Music Publishers Holding Corp.

PAGE MISS GLORY (*Film*):
Page Miss Glory (*Al Dubin*), Music Publishers Holding Corp.

SHIPMATES FOREVER (*Film*):
Don't Give up the Ship (*Al Dubin*), Music Publishers Holding Corp.
I'd Rather Listen to Your Eyes (*Al Dubin*), Music Publishers Holding Corp.
I'd Love to Take Orders from You (*Al Dubin*), Music Publishers Holding Corp.

STARS OVER BROADWAY (*Film*):
You Let Me Down (*Al Dubin*), Music Publishers Holding Corp.
At Your Service, Madame (*Al Dubin*), Music Publishers Holding Corp.
Where Am I? (*Al Dubin*), Music Publishers Holding Corp.
Broadway Cinderella (*Al Dubin*), Music Publishers Corp.

Octoroon (Instrumental)
Wail of the Winds (Instrumental)

1936

COLLEEN (*Film*):
You Gotta Know How to Dance (*Al Dubin*), Music Publishers Holding Corp.
Boulevadier from the Bronx (*Al Dubin*), Music Publishers Holding Corp.
An Evening with You (*Al Dubin*), Music Publishers Holding Corp.
I Don't Have to Dream Again (*Al Dubin*), Music Publishers Holding Corp.

HEARTS DIVIDED (*Film*):
Two Hearts Divided (*Al Dubin*), Music Publishers Holding Corp.
My Kingdom for a Kiss (*Al Dubin*), Music Publishers Holding Corp.

CAIN AND MABEL (*Film*):
Coney Island (*Al Dubin*), Music Publishers Holding Corp.
I'll Sing You a Thousand Love Songs (*Al Dubin*), Music Publishers Holding Corp.

SONS O' GUNS (*Film*):
For a Buck and a Quarter a Day (*Al Dubin*), Music Publishers Holding Corp.
In the Arms of an Army Man (*Al Dubin*), Music Publishers Holding Corp.

GOLD DIGGERS OF 1937 (*Film*):
With Plenty of Money and You (*Al Dubin*), Music Publishers Holding Corp.

All's Fair in Love and War (*Al Dubin*), Music Publishers Holding Corp.

SING ME A LOVE SONG (*Film*):
The Least You Can Do for a Lady (*Al Dubin*), Music Publishers Holding Corp.
Summer Night (*Al Dubin*), Music Publishers Holding Corp.
The Little House That Love Built (*Al Dubin*), Music Publishers Holding Corp.

1937

MARKED WOMAN (*Film*):
My Silver Dollar Man (*Al Dubin*), Music Publishers Holding Corp.

MELODY FOR TWO (*Film*):
Melody for Two (*Al Dubin*), Music Publishers Holding Corp.
September in the Rain (*Al Dubin*), Music Publishers Corp.

STOLEN HOLIDAY (*Film*):
Stolen Holiday (*Al Dubin*), Music Publishers Holding Corp.

THE SINGING MARINE (*Film*):
The Song of the Marines (*Al Dubin*), Music Publishers Holding Corp.
I Know Now (*Al Dubin*), Music Publishers Holding Corp.
The Lady Who Couldn't Be Kissed (*Al Dubin*), Music Publications Holding Corp.
'Cause My Baby Says It's So (*Al Dubin*), Music Publications Holding Corp.
You Can't Run Away from Love Tonight (*Al Dubin*), Music Publishers Holding Corp.
Night Over Shanghai (*Johnny Mercer*), Music Publishers Holding Corp.

SAN QUENTIN (*Film*):
How Could You? (*Al Dubin*), Music Publishers Holding Corp.

MR. DODD TAKES THE AIR (*Film*):
Remember Me? (*Al Dubin*), Music Publishers Holding Corp.
Am I in Love? (*Al Dubin*), Music Publishers Holding Corp.
Here Comes the Sandman (*Al Dubin*), Music Publishers Holding Corp.
The Girl You Used to Be (*Al Dubin*), Music Publishers Holding Corp.

1938

GOING PLACES (*Film*):
Jeepers Creepers (*Johnny Mercer*), Music Publishers Holding Corp.
Say It with a Kiss (*Al Dubin*), Music Publishers Holding Corp.

335

Oh, What a Horse Was Charlie (*Al Dubin*), Music Publishers Holding Corp.

JEZEBEL (*Film*):
Jezebel (*Johnny Mercer*), Music Publishers Holding Corp.

GOLD DIGGERS IN PARIS (*Film*):
A Stranger in Paree (*Al Dubin*), Music Publishers Holding Corp.
I Wanna Go Back to Bali (*Al Dubin*), Music Publishers Holding Corp.
The Latin Quarter (*Al Dubin*), Music Publishers Holding Corp.
Put That Down in Writing (*Al Dubin*), Music Publishers Holding Corp.
Daydreaming (All Night Long) (*Johnny Mercer*), Music Publishers Holding Corp.
My Adventure (*Johnny Mercer*), Music Publishers Holding Corp.

GARDEN OF THE MOON (*Film*):
Garden of the Moon (*Dubin and Mercer*), Music Publishers Holding Corp.
The Girl Friend of the Whirling Dervish (*Dubin and Mercer*), Music Publishers Holding Corp.
Love Is Where You Find It (*Dubin and Mercer*), Music Publishers Holding Corp.
The Lady on the Two-Cent Stamp (*Dubin and Mercer*), Music Publishers Holding Corp.
Confidentially (*Dubin and Mercer*), Music Publishers Holding Corp.

COWBOY FROM BROOKLYN (*Film*):
Cowboy from Brooklyn (*Johnny Mercer*), Music Publishers Holding Corp.

HARD TO GET (*Film*):
You Must Have Been a Beautiful Baby (*Johnny Mercer*), Music Publishers Holding Corp.
There's a Sunny Side to Every Situation (*Johnny Mercer*), Music Publishers Holding Corp.

Something Tells Me (*Johnny Mercer*), Music Publishers Holding Corp.
You're an Education (*Al Dubin*), Music Publishers Holding Corp.

1939
NAUGHTY BUT NICE (*Film*):
Corn Pickin' (*Johnny Mercer*), Music Publishers Holding Corp.
Hooray for Spinach (*Johnny Mercer*), Music Publishers Holding Corp.
I'm Happy about the Whole Thing (*Johnny Mercer*), Music Publishers Holding Corp.

In a Moment of Weakness (*Johnny Mercer*), Music Publishers Holding Corp.

WINGS OF THE NAVY (*Film*):
Wings over the Navy (*Johnny Mercer*), Music Publishers Holding Corp.

Tears from My Inkwell (*Mort Dixon*), Music Publishers Holding Corp.
Roller Skating on a Rainbow (*Billy Rose and Irving Kahal*), Bregman, Vocco and Conn Inc.
Somebody Nobody Knows (*Bud Green*), Green Bros. and Knight, Inc.

HONOLULU (*Film*):
Honolulu (*Gus Kahn*), Bregman, Vocco and Conn Inc.
The Leader Doesn't Like Music (*Gus Kahn*), Bregman, Vocco and Conn Inc.
This Night Will Be Our Souvenir (*Gus Kahn*), Bregman, Vocco and Conn Inc.

1940
Devil May Care (*Johnny Burke*), Music Publishers Holding Corp.
Huckleberry Man (*Ted Koehler*), Irving Berlin, Inc.

YOUNG PEOPLE (*Film*):
I Wouldn't Take a Million (*Mack Gordon*), Twentieth Century Music Corp.
Young People (*Mack Gordon*), Twentieth Century Music Corp.
Fifth Avenue (*Mack Gordon*), Twentieth Century Music Corp.
Tra-la-la (*Mack Gordon*), Twentieth Century Music Corp.

DOWN ARGENTINA WAY (*Film*):
Down Argentina Way (*Mack Gordon*), Robbins, Feist and Miller Corp.
Nenita (*Mack Gordon*), Robbins, Feist and Miller Corp.
Sing to Your Señorita (*Mack Gordon*), Robbins, Feist and Miller Corp.
Two Dreams Met (*Mack Gordon*), Robbins, Feist and Miller Corp.

TIN PAN ALLEY (*Film*):
You Say the Sweetest Things, Baby (*Mack Gordon*), Twentieth Century Music Corp.

1941
THAT NIGHT IN RIO (*Film*):
They Met in Rio (*Mack Gordon*), Robbins, Feist and Miller Corp.
I Yi Yi Yi Yi (*Mack Gordon*), Robbins, Feist and Miller Corp.

Chica Chica Boom Chic (*Mack Gordon*), Robbins, Feist and Miller Corp.

Bona Noite (*Mack Gordon*), Robbins, Feist and Miller Corp.

The Baron Is in Conference (*Mack Gordon*), Robbins, Feist and Miller Corp.

THE GREAT AMERICAN BROADCAST (*Film*):

The Great American Broadcast (*Mack Gordon*), Twentieth Century Music Corp.

It's All in a Lifetime (*Mack Gordon*), Twentieth Century Music Corp.

I Take to You (*Mack Gordon*), Twentieth Century Music Corp.

Long Ago Last Night (*Mack Gordon*), Twentieth Century Music Corp.

I've Got a Bone to Pick with You (*Mack Gordon*), Twentieth Century Music Corp.

Where Are You? (*Mack Gordon*), Twentieth Century Music Corp.

SUN VALLEY SERENADE (*Film*):

It Happened in Sun Valley (*Mack Gordon*), Twentieth Century Music Corp.

I Know Why (*Mack Gordon*), Twentieth Century Music Corp.

The Kiss Polka (*Mack Gordon*), Twentieth Century Music Corp.

Chattanooga Choo Choo (*Mack Gordon*), Twentieth Century Music Corp.

WEEKEND IN HAVANA (*Film*):

A Weekend in Havana (*Mack Gordon*), Bregman, Vocco and Conn. Inc.

When I Love, I Love (*Mack Gordon*), Bregman, Vocco and Conn. Inc.

The Nango (*Mack Gordon*),bregman, Vocco and Conn. Inc.

The Man with the Lollypop Song (*Mack Gordon*), Bregman, Vocco and Conn. Inc.

Tropical Magic (*Mack Gordon*), Bregman, Vocco and Conn. Inc.

The World Is Waiting to Waltz Again (*Mack Gordon*), Bregman, Vocco and Conn. Inc.

1942

American Barcarolle (Instrumental), Robbins Music Corp.

ORCHESTRA WIVES (*Film*):

That's Sabotage (*Mack Gordon*), Bregman, Vocco and Conn. Inc.

At Last (*Mack Gordon*), Bregman, Vocco and Conn. Inc.

People Like You and Me (*Mack Gordon*), Bregman, Vocco and Conn. Inc.

Serenade in Blue (*Mack Gordon*), Bregman, Vocco and Conn. Inc.

I've Got a Gal in Kalamazoo (*Mack Gordon*), Bregman, Vocco and Conn. Inc.

ICELAND (*Film*):

You Can't Say No to a Soldier (*Mack Gordon*), Edwin H. Morris, Inc.

Let's Bring New Glory to Old Glory (*Mack Gordon*), Edwin H. Morris, Inc.

There Will Never Be Another You (*Mack Gordon*), Edwin H. Morris, Inc.

It's the Lover's Knot (*Mack Gordon*), Edwin H. Morris, Inc.

I Like a Military Tune (*Mack Gordon*), Edwin H. Morris, Inc.

SPRINGTIME IN THE ROCKIES (*Film*):

I Had the Craziest Dream (*Mack Gordon*), Bregman, Vocco and Conn. Inc.

Pan American Jubilee (*Mack Gordon*), Bregman, Vecco and Conn. Inc.

A Poem Set to Music (*Mack Gordon*), Bregman, Vecco and Conn. Inc.

Run, Little Raindrop, Run (*Mack Gordon*), Twentieth Century Music Corp.

I Like to Be Loved by You (*Mack Gordon*), Twentieth Century Music Corp.

1943

HELLO, FRISCO, HELLO (*Film*):

You'll Never Know (*Mack Gordon*), Bregman, Vocco and Conn. Inc.

I Gotta Have You (*Mack Gordon*), Bregman, Vocco and Conn. Inc.

SWEET ROSIE O'GRADY (*Film*):

My Heart Tells Me (*Mack Gordon*), Bregman, Vocco and Conn. Inc.

My Sam (*Mack Gordon*), Bregman, Vocco and Conn. Inc.

The Wishing Waltz (*Mack Gordon*), Bregman, Vocco and Conn. Inc.

Get Your Police Gazette (*Mack Gordon*), Bregman, Vocco and Conn. Inc.

Going to the County Fair (*Mack Gordon*), Bregman, Vocco and Conn. Inc.

Where, Oh Where, Is the Groom? (*Mack Gordon*), Bregman, Vocco and Conn. Inc.

THE GANG'S ALL HERE (*Film*):

The Polka Dot Polka (*Leo Robin*), Bregman, Vocco and Conn. Inc.

You Discover You're in New York (*Leo Robin*), Bregman, Vocco and Conn. Inc.

The Lady in the Tutti-Frutti Hat (*Leo Robin*), Bregman, Vocco and Conn. Inc.

Minnie's in the Money (*Leo Robin*), Bregman, Vocco and Conn. Inc.

A Journey to a Star (*Leon Robin*), Bregman, Vocco and Conn. Inc.

Paducah (*Leo Robin*), Bregman, Vocco and Conn. Inc.

No Love, No Nothin' (*Leo Robin*), Bregman, Vocco and Conn. Inc.

Carnival (*Leo Robin*), Bregman, Vocco and Conn. Inc.

1944

Forget-Me-Nots in Your Eyes (*Edgar Leslie*), Triangle Music Corp.

You've Got Me Where You Want Me (*Johnny Mercer*), Four Jays Music Inc.

ZIEGFELD FOLLIES (*Film*):

There's Beauty Everywhere (*Arthur Freed*), Bregman, Vocco and Conn. Inc.

This Heart of Mine (*Arthur Freed*), Bregman, Vocco and Conn. Inc.

1945

BILLY ROSE'S DIAMOND HORSESHOE (*Film*):

I Wish I Knew (*Mack Gordon*), Bregman, Vocco and Conn. Inc.

In Acapulco (*Mack Gordon*), Bregman, Vocco and Conn. Inc.

Mink Lament (*Mack Gordon*), Bregman, Vocco and Conn. Inc.

The More I See You (*Mack Gordon*), Bregman, Vocco and Conn. Inc.

A Nickel's Worth of Jive (*Mack Gordon*), Bregman, Vocco and Conn. Inc.

Play Me an Old Fashioned Melody (*Mack Gordon*), Bregman, Vocco and Conn. Inc.

YOLANDA AND THE THIEF (*Film*):

Yolanda (*Arthur Freed*), Robbins, Feist and Miller Corp.

Angel (*Arthur Freed*), Robbins, Feist and Miller Corp.

Will You Marry Me? (*Arthur Freed*), Robbins, Feist and Miller Corp.

This Is the Day for Love (*Arthur Freed*), Robbins, Feist and Miller Corp.

Coffee Time (*Arthur Freed*), Four Jays Music Inc.

1946

Me and the Blues (*Ted Koehler*), Robbins

THE HARVEY GIRLS)*Film*):

On the Atchison, Topeka and the Santa Fe (*Johnny Mercer*), Robbins, Feist and Miller Inc.

Swing Your Partner Round and Round (*Johnny Mercer*), Robbins, Feist and Miller Inc.

Wait and See (*Johnny Mercer*), Robbins, Feist and Miller Inc.

Wild, Wild West (*Johnny Mercer*), Robbins, Feist and Miller Inc.

Oh, You Kid (*Johnny Mercer*), Robbins, Feist and Miller Corp.

In the Valley (*Johnny Mercer*), Robbins, Feist and Miller Corp.

It's a Great Big World (*Johnny Mercer*), Robbins, Feist and Miller Corp.

The Train Must Be Fed (*Johnny Mercer*), Robbins, Feist and Miller Corp.

The March of the Dogies (*Johnny Mercer*), Four Jays Music Inc.

My Intuition (*Johnny Mercer*), Four Jay Music Inc.

THREE LITTLE GIRLS IN BLUE (*Film*):

This is Always (*Mack Gordon*), Bregman, Vocco and Conn. Inc.

1947

Every So Often (*Johnny Mercer*), Robbins, Feist and Miller Corp.

Baby, Have You Got a Little Love to Spare? (*Ted Koehler*), Four Jays Music Inc.

The First Time I Kissed You (*Ralph Blane*), Robbins, Feist and Miller Corp.

1948

SUMMER HOLIDAY (*Film*):

Weary Blues (*Ralph Blane*), Robbins, Feist and Miller Corp.

Afraid to Fall in Love (*Ralph Blane*), Four Jays Music Inc.

The Stanley Steamer (*Ralph Blane*), Four Jays Music Inc.

All Hail to Danville High (*Ralph Blane*), Four Jays Music Inc.

Independence Day (*Ralph Blane*), Four Jays Music Inc.

Spring Isn't Everything (*Ralph Blane*), Four Jays Music Inc.

Our Home Town (*Ralph Blane*), Four Jays Music Inc.

The Sweetest Kid I Ever Saw (*Ralph Blane*), Four Jays Music Inc.

A Brave Heart (*Ralph Blane*), Four Jays Music Inc.

While the Men Are All Drinking (*Ralph Blane*), Four Jays Music Inc.

You're Next (*Ralph Blane*), Four Jays Music Inc.

1949

Great Guns (*Johnny Mercer*), Robbins, Feist and Miller Corp.

When Sally Walks Along Peacock Alley (*Johnny Mercer*), Bregman, Vocco and Conn. Inc.

Love Woke Me up This Morning (*Johnny Mercer*), Bregman, Vocco and Conn. Inc.

MY DREAM IS YOURS)*Film*):

My Dream Is Yours (*Ralph Blane*), Music Publishers Holding Corp.

Someone Like You (*Ralph Blane*), Music Publishers Holding Corp.

Tick, Tick, Tick (*Ralph Blane*), Music Publishers Holding Corp.

Freddie, Get Ready (*Ralph Blane*), Music Publishers Holding Corp.

Love Finds a Way (*Ralph Blane*), Music Publishers Holding Corp.

THE BARKLEYS OF BROADWAY (*Film*):

You'd Be Hard to Replace (*Ira Gershwin*), Robbins, Feist and Miller Corp.

Shoes with Wings On (*Ira Gershwin*), Four Jays Music Inc.

My One and Only Highland Fling (*Ira Gershwin*), Four Jays Music Inc.

A Weekend in the Country (*Ira Gershwin*), Four Jays Music Inc.

Swing Trot (*Ira Gershwin*), Four Jays Music Inc.

Manhattan Downbeat (*Ira Gershwin*), Four Jays Music Inc.

Bouncin' the Blues (*instrumental*), Four Jays Music Inc.

1950

PAGAN LOVE SONG (*Film*):

Why Is Love So Crazy? (*Arthur Freed*), Robins, Feist and Miller Corp.

The House of Singing Bamboo (*Arthur Freed*), Four Jays Music Inc.

The Sea of the Moon (*Arthur Freed*), Four Jays Music Inc.

Tahiti (*Arthur Freed*), Four Jays Music Inc.

Singing in the Sun (*Arthur Freed*), Four Jays Music Inc.

Here in Tahiti We Make Love (*Arthur Freed*), Four Jays Music Inc.

Etiquette (*Arthur Freed*), Four Jays Music Inc.

SUMMER STOCK (*Film*):

Dig, Dig, Dig, Dig for Your Supper (*Mack Gordon*), Robbins, Feist and Miller Corp.

You, Wonderful You (*Saul Chaplin and Jack Brooks*), Four Jays Music Inc.

Friendly Star (*Mack Gordon*), Robbins, Feist and Miller Corp.

Mem'ry Island (*Mack Gordon*), Four Jays Music Inc.

If You Feel Like Singing, Sing (*Mack Gordon*), Four Jays Music Inc.

Howdy Neighbor, Happy Harvest (*Mack Gordon*), Four Jays Music Inc.

1951

TEXAS CARNIVAL (*Film*):

Young Folks Should Get Married (*Dorothy Fields*), Four Jays Music Inc.

Whoa, Emma (*Dorothy Fields*), Four Jays Music Inc.

It's Dynamite (*Dorothy Fields*), Four Jays Music Inc.

1952

THE BELLE OF NEW YORK (*Film*):

When I'm Out with the Belle of New York (*Johnny Mercer*), Robbins, Feist and Miller Corp.

Seeing's Believing (*Johnny Mercer*), Robbins, Feist and Miller Corp.

Baby Doll (*Johnny Mercer*), Robbins, Feist and Miller Corp.

Oops! (*Johnny Mercer*), Robbins, Feist and Miller Corp.

Naughty but Nice (*Johnny Mercer*), Robbins, Feist and Miller Corp.

I Wanna Be a Dancin' Man (*Johnny Mercer*), Four Jays Music Inc.

I Love to Beat the Big Bass Drum (*Johnny Mercer*), Four Jays Music Inc.

A Bride's Wedding Day Song (*Johnny Mercer*), Four Jays Music Inc.

Bachelor Dinner Song (*Johnny Mercer*), Four Jays Music Inc.

SKIRTS AHOY!)*Film*):

I Get a Funny Feeling (*Ralph Blane*), Robbins, Feist and Miller Corp.

The Navy Waltz (*Ralph Blane*), Robbins, Feist, and Miller Corp.

What Good Is a Gal without a Guy? (*Ralph Blane*), Four Jays Music Inc.

Skirts Ahoy! (*Ralph Blane*), Four Jays Music Inc.

Hold Me Close to You (*Ralph Blane*), Four Jays Music Inc.

Glad to Have You Aboard (*Ralph Blane*), Four Jays Music Inc.

What Makes a Wave? (*Ralph Blane*), Four Jays Music Inc.

JUST FOR YOU (*Film*):

Just for You (*Leo Robin*), Famous Music Corp.

I'll Si, Si Ya in Bahia (*Leo Robin*), Famous Music Corp.

He's Just Crazy for Me (*Leo Robin*), Famous Music Corp.

Zing a Little Zong (*Leo Robin*), Famous Music Corp.

The Live Oak Tree (*Leo Robin*), Famous Music Corp.

Call Me Tonight (*Leo Robin*), Famous Music Corp.

On the Ten-Ten from Ten-Ten-Tennessee (*Leo Robin*), Famous Music Corp.

Checkin' My Heart (*Leo Robin*), Famous Music Corp.

The Maiden of Guadalupe (*Leo Robin*), Famous Music Corp.

The Ole Spring Fever (*Leo Robin*), Four Jays Music Inc.

A Flight of Fancy (*Leo Robin*), Four Jays Music Inc.

1953

THE CADDY (*Film*):

What Would You Do without Me? (*Jack Brooks*), Famous Music Inc.

You're the Right One (*Jack Brooks*), Famous Music Inc.

That's Amore (*Jack Brooks*), Famous Music Inc.

The Gay Continental (*Jack Brooks*), Famous Music Inc.

It Takes a Lot of Little Likes to Make One Big Love (*Jack Brooks*), Famous Music Inc.

It's a Whistlin' Kind of Mornin' (*Jack Brooks*), Famous Music Inc.

1954

I've Never Known a Night Like This (*Saxie Dowall*), Tin Pan Avenue Music Inc.

1955

The Legend of Wyatt Earp (*Television theme song*) (*Harold Adamson*)

ARTISTS AND MODELS (*Film*):

Artists and Models (*Jack Brooks*), Famous Music Corp.

The Bat Lady (*Jack Brooks*), Famous Music Corp.

Inamorata (*Jack Brooks*), Famous Music Corp.

The Lucky Song (*Jack Brooks*), Famous Music Corp.

When You Pretend (*Jack Brooks*), Famous Music Corp.

You Look So Familiar (*Jack Brooks*), Famous Music Corp.

THE ROSE TATTOO (*Film*):

The Rose Tattoo (*Jack Brooks*), Famous Music Corp.

MARTY (*Film*):

Hey, Marty (*Paddy Chayefsky*), Cromwell Music Inc.

1956

THE BIRDS AND THE BEES (*Film*):

The Same Thing Happens with the Birds and the Bees (*Mack David*), Famous Music Corp.

La Parisienne (*Mack David*), Famous Music Corp.

Each Time I Dream (*Mack David*), Famous Music Corp.

Little Miss Tippy-Toes (*Harold Adamson*), Four Jays Music Inc.

SHANGRI-LA (*Stage production*):

Lost Horizon (*Lawrence and Lee*), Edwin H. Morris Inc.

Second Time in Love (*Lawrence and Lee*) Edwin H. Morris Inc.

Shangri-La (*Lawrence and Lee*), Edwin H. Morris Inc.

1957

AN AFFAIR TO REMEMBER (*Film*):

An Affair To Remember (*Harold Adamson and Leo McCarey*), Famous Music Corp.

The Tiny Scout (*Harold Adamson and Leo McCarey*), Famous Music Corp.

Tomorrow Land (*Harold Adamson and Leo McCarey*), Famous Music Corp.

You Make It Easy to Be True (*Harold Adamson and Leo McCarey*), Famous Music Corp.

THE CALIFORNIANS (*Television production*):

I've Come To California (*Harold Adamson*), Four Jays Music Inc.

1958

ROCK-A-BYE BABY (*Film*):

Dormi, Dormi, Dormi (*Sammy Cahn*), Famous Music Corp.

Love Is a Lonely Thing (*Sammy Cahn*), Famous Music Corp.

Rock-a-bye Baby (*Sammy Cahn*), Famous Music Corp.

The Land of La La La (*Sammy Cahn*), Famous Music Corp.

The White Virgin of the Nile (*Sammy Cahn*), Famous Music Corp.

Why Can't He Care for Me? (*Sammy Cahn*), Famous Music Corp.

THESE THOUSAND HILLS (*Film*):
These Thousand Hills (*Ned Washington*), Robbins, Feist and Miller Inc.

SEPARATE TABLES (*Film*):
Separate Tables (*Harold Adamson*), Hecht-Lancaster Music Inc.

A Dream for a Lovely Night (*Mack David*), Edwin H. Morris Inc.

1959
Make Mine Love (*Harold Adamson*), Four Jays Music Inc.

1960
CINDERFELLA (*Film*):
Turn It On (*Jack Brooks*), Famous Music Corp.
Let Me Be a People (*Jack Brooks*), Famous Music Corp.
Somebody (*Jack Brooks*), Famous Music Corp.
The Other Fella (*Jack Brooks*), Famous Music Corp.
The Princess Waltz (*with Walter Scharf*), Famous Music Corp.

1961
THE LADIES' MAN (*Film*):
Don't Go to Paris (*Jack Brooks*), Famous Music Corp.
He Doesn't Know (*Jack Brooks*), Famous Music Corp.

1962
SATAN NEVER SLEEPS (*Film*):
Satan Never Sleeps (*Harold Adamson and Leo McCarey*), Robbins, Feist and Miller Corp.

I Wonder What It's Like to Be In Paris (*Harry Warren*), Four Jays Music Inc.
Have a Drink on Me (*Harry Warren*), Four Jays Music Inc.

1963
Helpless (*Hal Shaper*), Four Jays Music Inc.

1964
Miss Oklahoma (*Ralph Blane*), Four Jays Music Inc.
You're the Girl for Me (*Ralph Blane*), Four Jays Music Inc.

1967
Rosie (*Johnny Mercer*), Shamley Music Corp.
Golden Voyage (*Adam West*), Four Jays Music Inc.

1968
Finale (*Leo Robin*), Four Jays Music Inc.

1969
I Just Stood and Stared (*Richard O. Kraemer*), Leo Feist Inc.
The Miracle of Spring (*Richard O. Kraemer*), Leo Feist Inc.

1970
Jethro and Jezebelle (*Richard O. Kraemer*), Four Jays Music Inc.
The Way It Was (*Richard O. Kraemer*), Four Jays Music Inc.
The Magic's Missing (*Richard O. Kraemer*), Four Jays Music Inc.
I Got the Message (*Richard O. Kraemer*), Leo Feist Inc.

ADDENDUM:

Mr. Warren's own publishing company, Four Jays Music Co. Inc., 1610 North Argyle Avenue, Hollywood, California 90028, controls the songs published by Harry Warren Music Inc., in association with Metro-Goldwyn-Mayer, including those which were deleted from films. Four Jays is also the publisher of Mr. Warren's *Piano Vignettes*, a group of instrumental pieces: "Autumn Reverie," "Blue Midnight," "Boarding House Blues," "Carioca Capers," "Down Town Blues," "Gee Willikens," "Kelly Green," "Le Petit Trianon," "Moods," "Moon Mist," "Night Jasmine," "Parade of the Penguins," "Portraits," "Reflections," "Silhouettes," "Stumbling Blocks," "Sunday in the City," "Talking Tango," "The Dell," "The Red Shawl," and "The Spanish Dancer."

INDEX

342

344